"Living as if your life really matters takes conscious thoughts, words, and deeds. John St. Augustine is one of the few people on the planet who lives consciously—and gets the most out of his life by extracting the hidden treasures so many of us miss. *Every Moment Matters* will wake you up, shake you up, and take you up to the next level of awareness so your burdens become blessings and challenges become cause for celebration."

JEAN CHATZKY
Best-selling author of *The Difference*
Financial Editor of *The Today Show*, NBC

. . . .

"What a magical book. Each chapter contains a compelling story that slowly unfolds into a life lesson we can all benefit from. While reading, I laughed and cried and had myself many great 'moments.' It's a gem of a book—one that you'll want to share with those who help you create the most important moments of all—the people who truly matter."

CHERYL RICHARDSON
Best-selling author of *The Art of Extreme Self Care*
and *The Unmistakable Touch of Grace*

. . . .

"*Every Moment Matters* is a cherished gem. John St. Augustine's powerful and uplifting stories lift the soul, fill the heart, and expand the mind. A perfect tonic for our radically changing times."

WILLIAM L. MURTHA
Author of *Dying for a Change* and
Visionaries for the 21st Century

. . . .

"A close brush with death—or such an experience by a dearly loved one—makes it very clear that each day, all the hours—indeed, every minute—in our lives is an unparalleled gift. Yet how to make the most of every one? Now comes this very special book by John St. Augustine, giving us a wonderful insight into the breathtaking treasure that is Every Moment. Nothing will put you back in touch with the wonder of life faster than this book!"

NEALE DONALD WALSCH
Best-selling author of *Conversations with God*

every moment matters

savoring the stuff of life

John St. Augustine

HAMPTON ROADS
PUBLISHING COMPANY, INC.

Cover design by Gopa & Ted2 Inc.
Cover photograph © Jupiterimages Unlimited

Hampton Roads Publishing Company, Inc.
www.hrpub.com

Library of Congress Cataloging-in-Publication Data
is available upon request.

ISBN 978-1-57174-589-7

10 9 8 7 6 5 4 3 2 1
Printed on acid-free paper in Canada

To Amanda Lee and Andrew John

For teaching me that every moment matters . . .

Contents

Foreword

As a surgeon and scientist, it has been my life's calling to become a student of the human heart and all the nuances, emotions, and physical structures that make this organ the most important of all human hardware, the very sustainer of life. From the *moment* your heart starts beating (just about twenty-one days after you were conceived) to the *moment* you take your last breath (about seventy-seven years later, give or take), your heart has given you the greatest gift imaginable: *life*. And all without you ever giving it a single conscious command to pump oxygen-rich blood through your circulatory system. It keeps you alive because it feeds itself first.

This book is also about feeding yourself first. John St. Augustine is a friend, mentor, and formidable voice in the world who has a gift. He sees things most of us miss, the sacred spaces that are hidden in the ordinary events of life and the lessons contained in those events that make life more vibrant and worth living. John invites us to share spaces from his journey—one forged from his relentless quest to squeeze as much out of being alive as possible, be it climbing to a mountaintop in Colorado or walking a thousand miles in search of his higher self or donating a kidney to save his daughter's life. He sees our existence as not just a life of work, but rather a work of art and invites us to create a canvas that reflects the short time we have on Earth as one of awareness, service, joy, and giving—all tempered with a measured dose of urgency, for tomorrow is promised to no one.

From this *moment* on, you can alter your life for the better in so many different ways—by changing your diet, doing regular exercise, and having a positive outlook on the world you inhabit. All those things and more can help keep you from having to see someone like me with a mask on my face and scalpel in hand. Prevention is always the best prescription. It's often not until we are faced with nature's wake-up call disguised as a "life threatening" illness that we begin to become fully alive and smell the roses that have been there all along—just out of reach as we fill our lives with things that seem to have great meaning at the time but little meaning in the long run. I know better than most that someday even the miraculous heart ceases its offerings, and in that *moment,* life ends. You can begin now to give your heart perhaps the most important thing it needs—a reason to keep beating—and it starts by knowing that *Every Moment Matters.*

MEHMET C. OZ, MD, host of *The Dr. Oz Show,*
author of the YOU! health book series

Preface

It will be many months before you read these words written at 4:44 Eastern Standard Time on a cool and very dark June morning when I just could not sleep. It might have been my sixteen-year-old son and his buddies laughing like the Three Stooges in the basement at one in the morning or the fact that every day is a new adventure when it comes to being the parent of an eighteen-year-old daughter who has discovered that staying out until three-thirty in the morning is a sure way to keep her parents from getting *too* much sleep. Or it could be that I spent most of my Saturday with about two feet between my nose and the trillions of flowers and weeds that call my northern Michigan backyard home, which no amount of over-the-counter anything can help. But, truth be told, it was the graduation party that started all that follows in these pages.

As I sit in the den and look to my right at the table covered with volleyball trophies, framed awards, and a stand-up "picture board," it reminds me that eighteen years have passed since my daughter arrived and sixteen years since her brother made his entrance. Nestled behind the diploma and letter of acceptance to college is a stark reminder that "Kodak Moments" are truly the stuff of life. There is the shot of my daughter just a few days old, curled up on her mother's chest as they both slept on the couch in our first apartment . . . click . . . she is two years old and surrounded by a mountain of pumpkins for Halloween . . . click . . . the girl is a star softball player at ten (with her own trading card to prove it) and holds the bat like it's her only time at the plate . . . click . . . thirteen has come around, and her school picture shows a gaunt face but a fierce intensity in her eyes, as it will be just months before I donate a kidney to save her life . . . click . . . she stands with three other kids in front of the lake dressed for prom and looking like a model with the words "Love Is Forever" imprinted on the photo. The images all begin to blend into one . . . time passes.

My sight is drawn to more images standing on my roll-top desk. There are Jackie and I more than ten years earlier in a somewhat uncertain embrace as I showed up where she worked, just a few moments removed from the walk I took from Upper Michigan to Chicago and back—a journey I had to take to remember who I am, but which strained our relationship far past "for better or for worse." The frame next to it holds the image of my father on the day he graduated from high school in 1953. The look in his eyes is one of readiness, as if he were poised to seize the next moment and squeeze it for all it is worth. I was not even a thought in his mind. It has been four years since he passed and more than ten since my mother has been gone, neither of them here to be a part of the family photo taken after today's graduation.

In preparation for putting together the "picture board," the battered Rubbermaid container was pulled out, filled to bursting with thousands more sobering reminders that I am not the whippy-wristed, flat-bellied, "put-your-ears-back-and-go-get-'em stud muffin" I once was. While photographs can be fun to look at—and may be the most significant evidence humans have created—too many images to count prove once and for all that time is not on our side when it comes to creating a life based on inspiration, not desperation.

My steadfast writing partner, Cleo the cat, keeps a safe distance from the balloons attached to the six yellow roses commemorating the event. The balloons sway slightly in the breeze that works its way inside through the open kitchen window and offers the first fragrance of morning. My mind wanders to the previous night: I watched my daughter walk across the stage to receive her high-school diploma, looking radiant and healthy nearly five years post-kidney transplant. My mind suddenly raced further back . . . thirty years . . . to the very same moment I crossed a stage—scroll in one hand, handshake in the other—toward an uncertain tomorrow. In the roughly 11,950 days that have seemingly evaporated since that evening, I cannot help but wonder where time has gone. What have I done with the moments that have been given to me? What do I have to show for it? What lessons have I learned? What legacy will I leave behind, if any? Am I evolving or revolving? Have I squeezed the life out of the moments life has offered?

So off I go to the keyboard once again, and this time out of the literary chute flow words about the one thing we cherish the most and wish we had more of. Money? Nope. Sex . . . hmm. No again. How about education or vacations or love or sleep or a larger network of people or better seats at the ballgame or free cellphone minutes? Sorry, no to all of the above.

Let me give you a hint: It's a very simple thing, and I have already alluded to it twice before this sentence. It is often transparent and empty, waiting to be filled. It's sometimes loud and scary and exhil-arating, over the top with energy and chaos. No idea yet?

Here is what the all-knowing and all-seeing *Webster's Dictionary* has to say about this "thing," for lack of a better term: a) the mean of the nth powers of the deviations of the observed values in a set of statistical data from a fixed value; b) the expected value of a power of the deviation of a random variable from a fixed value. Nothing yet? How about this: a) tendency or measure of tendency to produce motion especially about a point or axis; b) the product of quantity (as a force) and the distance to a particular axis or point. No? I didn't get it either. Getting irritated? Okay, here you go. This entire book is dedicated to a minute portion or point of time; a time of excellence or conspicuousness; importance in influence or effect <a matter of great *moment*>.

Now, that last definition must have caught your attention, at least a little. *A matter of great moment . . .* Great moments matter . . . and so do not-so-great moments, and small moments, and quiet moments, and life-changing moments, and shitty moments, and, of course, Kodak Moments.

As I sit in the presence of the new day, the horizon turning from deep, dark blue to lighter shades of gray, I take note of the fact that morning has once again arrived right on time and that it does so without anyone's permission. This ancient process does not happen all at once, but rather . . . in a series of *moments.*

But even *Webster's,* in all its depth, cannot accurately describe a moment. You can do something at "the spur of the moment" or have "a moment of truth" or even be asked to "wait just a moment," but these are just small words working really hard to convey a very big gift.

Moments fascinate me because we all have them. Can it be that our lives are nothing more than a "string of moments" held together by our "experience" of them? The answer is a resounding . . . *maybe.* I would say yes based on my lifetime, but for some reason not everyone agrees. Some people feel that life (a string of moments bound together) is a burden, something to be dragged around from one day into the next, and that the next moment holds no promise, no magic or meaning. Perhaps they have watched too many news stories that hold the spotlight on the lowest of human behavior and have concluded that it's easier to withdraw from life than to engage in it fully. The magic of life has been slowly beaten out of them by a narrow, myopic view of the world they live in.

However, more and more of us are waking up from our consumer-driven comas as our economic woes reflect our collective attempt to buy, mortgage, and invest our way into some sense of self-worth. We are starting to realize that the promises made by our techno-driven world are hollow at best, not to mention short-lived. The minute our cellphones or PDAs become "obsolete," our sense of self takes a hit, and we rush out to buy a "better" one to keep up with the rat race—only to find out we are still rats . . . with more stuff. A fellow whom I work with saw my battered, three-year-old cellphone (that works just fine) and told me I should buy a new one. When I asked why, he said, "Because yours looks outdated." With that response, I knew he had been drinking the "*cool*-ade."

But a small voice inside that has been long ignored beckons us to mind our own business as our billions of miles of brain circuits are drenched with the latest news of celebrities and others who have fallen off the wagon—or been run over by one. A great long-ing is urging us to take the road less traveled and find out the truth before the sands of life run through the hourglass of time. More than ever before, we are in search of our "true selves," which have been long covered up by all the "right" things in life, according to society's measure—houses, cars, watches, clothes, whatever. You know, all the stuff that ends up in either a garage sale or an "estate" sale, depending on how much your surviving relatives feel like spending on advertising. And be clear about one thing: the powers-that-be—those who insist on diverting our attention from the inside to the outside and do not want you to wake up and think for yourself—are not the least bit interested in you unhooking yourself from the life-support system that keeps you running like your life solely depends on what you have. It's an amazing thing, really. The farther you get from the false promises of the world, the closer you get to the truth of who you truly are—*and can be.*

I offer this book as a prescription for the way out of this maze of materialism, media influence, and monetary madness. As I continue to be a keen observer of my own existence, one thing becomes crystal clear: while the journey has been one of discipline and self-examination, with some great success and even greater disappointments, my life (and I suspect yours, too) is filled with moments that changed me. They taught me something, made me stop alive in my tracks, had me catch my breath, or just plain made me glad to be alive or question my entire existence. While we can look to those moments as life altering, it is only upon further inspection that the teachings come forth, the foundation upon which we build our tomorrows.

I feel like the great author John Steinbeck when he crisscrossed America in 1960 and wrote *Travels with Charley,* his reflections on life, liberty, and the pursuit of happiness in "new America" with his standard poodle, Charley. I was two when he wrote the book, and I have a cat named Cleo, but we do have one other thing in common besides our first name: Steinbeck took the trip because he knew he was dying and wanted to see his country one last time. Well, I have a confession to make. I, too, am dying. My days are numbered. There is a beginning date of December 29, 1958, and the expiration on this model is somewhere encoded in my physical and spiritual DNA. And so it is with you, as well. Don't get fooled into thinking that because your picture is not in today's obit page that you will get out of life alive. If you feel that way, then some serious deprogramming needs to take place, and Madison Avenue has its hooks in you deeper than I thought. Time for a little reality check: *You're going to die, just like the rest of us.* But the good news is that you can make an important decision right now: *to really live, like only a few of us.*

This seems to be the most appropriate space to make clear a few notions about this work. I tend to scribe in a circular fashion, not linear. That is to say, a few events and people I will touch on in this book have appeared in my previous book, *Living an Uncommon Life,* as I recall moments that are nudging to be noticed and be revisited once again—coming full circle, as it were. I would also like to state that these events are from my point of view. No matter how thin you slice a tomato, there are always two sides. Thus, if you are offended by something I have written or a stance I take or even take issue with the way that it's being offered, then there is a 100 percent chance that whatever is pushing your buttons is most likely that thing you need to change the most. At least, that is what this author has learned about his life experience up to this point.

On another note, there are no "follow these rules for a better life" points in this book. I am sure that my publisher and I will have a verbal tug-of-war over this, but for me the lessons, insights, or teachings need not be spelled out for you. I have left them buried within each chapter for you to discover on your own and in your own way, just as I had to extract them for myself. As it has been said, "Another may teach or tell you, but you have to do the work yourself." Life is interesting that way. The lesson always follows the moment or event. You don't get to study in preparation prior to a life-changing moment. It's only after you have lived through it that the teaching becomes apparent.

The words of Chief Joseph were on me when I sat down to write. "It does not require many words to speak the truth." Life is a busy place in the twenty-first century, so condensing fifty years into bite-sized bits was challenging. But if your days are like mine, this retrospective is just the right size, even if I had to chop, cut, paste, and trim to make it fit.

It didn't hurt *too* much.

So this, then, is a journal of moments—a sampling of times that really stung me and those that challenged me. Many defined me and still more broke me down in order to build me up. A few even changed my world forever, along with the teachings that accompanied them, just to make sure I do not spend time repeating them over and over again. I have experienced some unexpected emotions as I relived many of these moments while putting pen to paper. "God bumps," shedding tears, and grinding my teeth in response to events that now only live in my mind tell me that while the physical moment may pass, the emotional umbilical cord to those times remains intact. We have been instructed by our modern-day mentors to "live in the moment." Since "now" is all that exists, then living in it is fairly simple. Staying in it, however, is a little more difficult. It's okay to let in a little of yesterday if it enhances the moments you have today.

So as the coffee kicks in and the half-eaten sandwich to my left begs my attention, my only intention is that you put down this book (after reading it cover to cover) and realize the potent nucleus that you are. Each and every moment is like a still pond, waiting for you to become a part of it and create a ripple effect that sends concentric rings into the furthermost reaches of your sacred experience of life. It starts with living as if every moment matters.

Many Thanks . . .

When your first book comes out, you thank a kazillion people. The second time around, you thank a little fewer than that. So, here goes, and if I left you out, know that I am thinking about you. Writing, for the most part, is a solo sport, but nothing is ever accomplished alone.

Many thanks to my family, as always, for their love and support when I am bent unflinchingly over the keyboard for hours while life goes on around me: Jackie, Amanda, and Andrew . . . and Cleo the cat.

Ginny Weissman has been a friend, manager, and adviser for years; a supporter and official "nudger" when it comes to making sure I finish the book, respond to an email, or get to an interview or event on time. Anna May Sims counsels from the coast and is always on target. Daryn Kagan often reminds me to trust the process, and Dr. Kelly Johnson continues to be steadfast in his support of my radio voice. TJ Ryan is always there when I need him, along with Hal Thau, who has told me for years that who I am and what I do make the world a better place. What we see in others, we have in ourselves, so right back at you, Hal.

The spirit of this book, along with the stories and lessons, could not be shared without a certain type of energy. Four women in particular—Annie Denver, Dr. Kathleen Hall, Catherine Crier, and Cheryl Richardson—are keepers of that energy. Thanks for sending some of it my way right when I need it most. Deep thanks to Bettie Youngs for her continued support and Susan Heim for her editing expertise. Thanks also to Dr. Mike Roizen, a true gentleman, and my spiritual sister, Libby Moore.

Up north, a whole group of incredible people allows me to vent, drink gallons of "truth serum" (coffee), and then sweat it out. Without them, this book would not exist. Thanks to Bruce and Pat Hardwick, Duane and Carol Kinnart, Dave and Vita Cobb, Doug and Robin Hewitt, Dennis and Kathy Wotchko, Bud and Deb Nedeau, Rolf and Renata Winters, Van Archiquette, and Annie Baum.

The walk would not be the same without the mentors in my life. They check in on me from time to time and always leave me with a lesson learned: Jerry Kramer, James Amos Jr., the late great Rev. Bob G. Sills, Prof. Dan Creely Jr., and Kevin Creely. On the other side of the chromosomes, Sharon "The Hobbit" Hogue never cuts me any slack, and I appreciate it. Esateys teaches the lesson of focus, Suzy Jordan is my biggest cheerleader, and Jennifer Weigel reminds me to push the envelope. Lisa Oz provides a new perspective just when I need it.

Three incredible humans with whom I have had the privilege to work and grow over the years remind me that friendship and careers often look like the same thing. I have concluded that Dr. Mehmet Oz is such an amazing heart surgeon because his own heart is the source of healing for those who are ill, less fortunate, or seeking to improve their lives, and I am deeply grateful for his words in the foreword of this book. Bob Greene has given me some of the best ab-building exercises ever, in the form of laughter—on and off the air. Thanks BG! Last but not least, my gratitude extends to the friend with whom I spend the most time in regards to radio and the one who has shown me courage and persistence above and beyond the call of duty . . . Ms. Jean Chatzky.

I have had the privilege of working with some of the best that radio has to offer, and while I could say something special about each one of them, the bottom line is that this group took the Oprah Radio concept and made it reality: Erik Logan, John Gehron, Laurie Cantillo, Johnny Keith, Corny Koehl, Mark Ruffin, Mr. Scott Miller, Ms. Rita Whack, "Doctor" Scott Clifton, Matt "Sparky" Comings, Rita Thomas, Geneen Harston, April "Mac" Davis, Lesley Martin, Katie B, "Marley," JJ Miller, Alicia Haywood, Rob "Broadway" Fagin (the one who really holds all this together), and, of course, the one and only Katherine Kelly.

Many thanks to my team, which puts up with my lack of technical understanding, missed meetings and emails, not to mention occasional bouts of Frankie Valli music blaring from my office, and keeps me going: the person who adds to and never takes away, Teresa Rodriguez; my radio right arm, Tiffany Square; and one call does it all, Katie Gibson; along with Charles the Lawyer and George Burns, with big-time thanks to Dr. Robin Smith, Peter Walsh, Marianne Williamson, Nate Berkus, and Ms. Gayle King (from your reluctant fan). Wayne Dyer's friendship has been of utmost importance.

A serious shout-out to my friend, Abe Thompson, for his unending faith in my radio presence over the years, and to Ms. Oprah Winfrey for the opportunity . . . I deeply appreciate it.

And thanks to you for reading this book.

— 1 —
Big Jake

What is it about our furred and feathered friends that gets so inside us? Perhaps it's an ancient connection from a time when the only thing between our ancestors and being the next meal for a saber-toothed tiger was a barking dog. Maybe it's the majesty of the pharaohs and the godlike qualities assigned to the forbears of the common housecat that bring a little royalty into our otherwise drab existence. For dog people, it's coming home and knowing that, no matter how your day went, Rover will accept you just the way you are. For cat lovers, it might be their air of aristocracy that makes us feel a little royal when we need it most. My life has been filled with great animal friends and guides, and I am a better human because of those that swim, crawl, walk, and fly. In particular, a very large boxer named Jake gave me some incredible moments.

I knew it the moment my eyes connected with those brown orbs behind the steel bars that he was coming home with me. The cage was in the corner of the living room. The woman was explaining to me that he was kept in this small prison most of the time because she had two little kids, and the dog was her husband's idea. A couple of bags of cheap dog food in the kitchen alluded to his bony condition, and as we spoke, it felt like this beautiful brindle boxer, with the pointed ears and stub for a tail, was silently pleading for me to set him free. Being a maverick myself, I understood his distaste for confinement, and I thought about how everything had lined up to make this happen. It was just a week earlier when I had called a shelter about the possibility of someone giving up a boxer for adoption. At first, the woman laughed at the thought of a purebred being let go for the cost of shots or a donation to the shelter. But as with things that are meant to be, there he was not five feet away, waiting for someone to come.

"So you will take Jake and give him a good home?" the woman asked tentatively, as she held one of her kids. The other one was using a chair for a diving board into the couch.

"Why do you call him Jake?" I asked.

"Nine months ago, when we brought him home, the movie *Big Jake* with John Wayne was on, and it seemed to fit." I wasn't sure if it was the dog's features or his swagger that resembled The Duke, but either way, the name had a ring to it.

"I will make sure that Jake has a great life," I replied. And with that the cage was opened, the prisoner was set free, and out the door we went. I had taken the back seat out of my Jeep and piled it with blankets in anticipation of this event, and in one graceful bound, Jake found his place in my truck and in my heart.

I watched him in the mirror as we drove back to the city. He was curled up in the same fashion as in the cage; for such a big dog, he had learned to become very small. The whole time we drove, he did not move and kept his brown eyes fixed on me. I felt like I had saved not only his life but also mine somehow. I was all of twenty-two years young at the time, proudly serving in the aviation wing of the United States Coast Guard. I was the quintessential All-American, with blond hair, blue eyes, a square jaw, and a life filled with sports and adventure. It seemed fitting that I have a dog that would somehow round out my existence. I was living with a young woman and had cleared the way for the possibility that I would be coming home with a dog. The landlord was a little harder to convince, and I think it was my volunteering to add fifty bucks to the rent each month that helped him say yes. As we bounced along the road to Chicago, I knew somehow deep inside that Jake was here to stay.

He took to the small two-room apartment in quick fashion, checking out every nook and cranny. I had not asked if he was housebroken, and it took less than five minutes to find out when he decided the file cabinet in the corner looked like a fire hydrant. We decided that the second bedroom would be his, and we set up a dog bed and feeding area, along with an assortment of things to keep him busy, such as rubber balls, a chew bone the size of a baseball bat, latex pull toys, and an old towel. As night drew near, Jake was the king of the castle. There were no steel bars to keep him from wandering his domain and nothing but love from his subjects, mainly me. The first night, Jake slept quietly on his throne as if he had been there forever. However, I was soon to find out that not every night would be like this one.

While I had cleared Jake off base, I still had to find a way to have him with me on the base, and that was going to take some time. So I walked him twice before I left for the day, made sure that he had plenty of food and water, and gave him free rein of the apartment. This went pretty well for a couple of weeks outside of the occasional deposit on the floor or chewed magazine in the rack—just normal dog stuff. All that came to a screeching halt one night.

I had parked my truck on the street in front of the apartment about a half-block down from where I lived. As I got out and began to walk toward the front door, I could hear a sound that was a cross between thunder and the vibration a saw makes when in the hands of a master player. Just as I reached the corner of the building, I looked up to the second floor where we lived. The huge plate-glass front window was bouncing like a trampoline! Not good. I bounded up the stairs and opened the door just in time to see Jake sprinting at full speed in a circle, using the three walls and front window as launch points for his act. He was in full gallop when I entered and yelled, "JAKE!" The boxer took one last leap off the far wall, spun into the middle of the room like some hairy circus acrobat, and stopped dead in his tracks, panting and drooling, with a look of exhaustion on his mug. I surveyed the damage.

The three giant plants my girlfriend had been growing for the past couple of years were totally dug up and out of their pots, and most of the dirt from them had been pushed into a pile under the corner of the rug, making a considerable bulge. Every magazine was out of the rack and either chewed on or drooled on, topped off with toilet paper that Jake had somehow managed to pull all the way into the living room without breaking it as it was still connected to the roll. The two designer pillows on the couch had become punching bags and had only half their stuffing. The rest of it was strewn about on the floor like snow. Various items from the garbage littered the hallway, indicating that the carnage also included the kitchen.

As I waded through the living room with my jaw hanging open in amazement, Jake plopped down smack dab in the middle of the mess and fell asleep. I turned the corner and peeked into the kitchen. The garbage can had been knocked over and spilled onto the floor. Somehow, Jake had managed to open the cabinets under the sink. He had then proceeded to pull out a squirt bottle of lighter fluid I kept for barbecuing, sunk his teeth into it, and shaken the flammable liquid out all over the walls. Other items that did not escape intact included a half-eaten box of SOS pads, four or five rubber gloves, and an entire bottle of laundry detergent that was leaking in the corner. I hesitated to inspect the premises further, but knew that with less than an hour to clean up, I needed to get moving.

The bathroom just had a couple of towels on the floor, and my bedroom door had been closed, which left Jake's room the only remaining property. The door was half-closed, and I timidly opened it fully and flipped on the light. *Holy crap.* The two sliding doors on the closet were knocked in, and four or five pairs of shoes were pulled out, half of them chewed to bits. Both filing cabinets were on their sides. The inside information remained safe from the marauding canine, but ample scratch marks indicated that Jake had given it his all. Pencils were chomped, rulers were wrecked, and calendars were crushed on impact. To top it all off, the only things untouched in the room were, of course, the doggie toys.

I failed to clean, replace, and reconstruct the apartment before my girlfriend got home. It's tough to wipe out the smell of lighter fluid once it has seeped into the rug, and no matter how much I fluffed the pillows, there was just not enough fluff to go around. The plants got back into their respective pots, but for the rest of it, a large garbage bag was the best recourse. A week or so prior to the explosion, I had traded in my Jeep for a Dodge pickup with a cab on the back, and while Jake (and I) were filled with remorse, he was banished to the back of the vehicle for the rest of the night. I threw in a couple of blankets and some chow that would keep him busy. I had not been in the apartment more than five minutes when I heard "Wooooo . . . wooooooooooooooo!" Jake was expressing his displeasure by doing what his ancestors had done for centuries: howling at the moon or, at least, me.

I resisted the inevitable trip down the block as long as possible, until I was convinced that he was going to howl until either I showed up or the neighbors called the cops. I went bounding out of bed, down the hallway, and down the street at near midnight, intent on keeping him quiet. No such luck. After what I thought was a reasonable request, filled with promises of dog treats if he was good and the threat of banishment to some far-off dog work camp if he wasn't, I watched him slowly fall asleep, apparently worn out from a full day of damage and howling. I closed the cab door, walked back to my apartment, and fell asleep. The silence lasted maybe six minutes. *THAT'S IT!* I thought. I grabbed a newspaper and rolled it up to swat the howler, flew down the stairs, out the door, and down the block. I yanked open the cab door and, in one fell swoop, took a swing at Jake's hindquarters. He was only a foot away, but he somehow felt the blow coming, and moved in the nick of time. I missed him entirely and only succeeded in jamming two fingers into the metal of the side of the truck. Now I was the one howling . . . in pain!

Jake cowered in the corner of the truck, sensing that somehow his vocal efforts had caused this. I surveyed the situation. *If I leave him out here, he is going to howl all night; I can't bring him in because my girlfriend would be one unhappy camper.* There was only one choice. I snuck back into the apartment, grabbed a couple of blankets and a pillow, and proceeded to join my furry friend in his mobile motel room on a Chicago side street in the middle of the night. Good thing it was summer. Strangely, that night was a preview of things to come.

Eventually, Jake made it on the airbase and became a bit of a mascot, with full rein to come and go as he pleased. It was always a great sight to see him take off in a full sprint in chase of a softball that had been hit or find him sleeping on top of a "mule" (the small, heavy-duty tractors we used to push and pull helicopters out of the hangar). He walked the parking lot and hallways as the undisputed lord of the manor, and we spent many a summer's day just hanging out as only man and dog can do. My picture had become complete, but it didn't last as long as I had hoped. My girlfriend and I went our separate ways, with me moving to the base temporarily and, more specifically, to the back of my truck at night to sleep while waiting for base housing. There we were, the two of us for an entire summer and part of the fall, in my Dodge Power Wagon, sleeping side by side. While it was a stressful time, looking back now, I realize I loved it. And so did Jake.

We bounced around a bit, and with just about a year to go on my enlistment, I really needed to clear my head about future plans. I decided to go to Colorado to visit an aunt (a story you will find in this book as well). With a heavy heart and impending changes in my life that did not seem to include my now 110-pound boxer, I found a family to take him while I went away and, if it worked out, forever. The day I dropped him off, one of their kids was having a birthday party in the yard, and I clearly remember walking Jake back to the event, making small talk with the new owners who assured me they were thrilled to have him, and then slowly backing out the way I came in. I watched Jake romping with the kids, eating cake, and chasing balloons. Once I hit the gangway, I turned and hurried down the path, unable to see the next step for the tears that poured down my face. At that point, he had not been away from my side for four years, and I felt like a part of me had been torn away.

I followed my plans for Colorado, knowing that Jake was in good hands, but it was a phone call from my sister on the second-to-last day of my trip that got me on the next flight back to Chicago. "The people that have Jake said if you don't come and get him, they are going have him sent to a kennel or put to sleep. He won't stop howling, and they can't handle him." Part of me smiled inside, but another part thought, *What am I going to do with him?* I retrieved Jake from the family, he took his proper place in the back of my Jeep, and we made do together until my enlistment ended (which brought a new set of challenges). I had talked with my parents, and they agreed I could stay back at the ranch until I found work or went back to finish my degree, but Jake was not an option. My mother had more cats than I could count and an aging Lab with horrible hips. Last thing they wanted was a howling hundred-pound-plus bundle of muscle and energy.

So, for the second time in less than a year, Jake was given a new home, picked up by a woman who professed to be a boxer aficionado. It lasted less than three days, and he was back with me in my old bedroom. We both promised the folks we would be good, and that I would replace anything he might devour (cats excepted). It was as if Jake was finally home. He became the willing target for the cat army as they launched attacks from all sides, but he knew his superior size and power had to be kept in check as they toyed with him. Jake and the Lab, "O-G," were reluctant housemates, with Jake deferring to the old man when it came to food and water and who ate first. As the Lab grew older and feebler, it was Jake who stood guard over him in case any intruder (real or imagined) would disturb his sleep. When O-G's time came to go across the Rainbow Bridge, Jake slumped around the house for weeks. In time, he took his place at the foot of my dad's chair.

Eventually, my life changed dramatically, as I got married and the kids arrived. I would see Jake whenever I could, and we would take walks up and down the block just like we did years earlier. As Jake's twelfth year rolled around, he had trouble walking and holding his bowels, and the decision I dreaded had to be made. It was time.

We went to the forest preserve first, and as best he could, Jake went from tree to tree and even made an attempt to gallop across a field like he did our first summer together at the airbase. I gave him a few bites of his favorite human food—doughnuts—and finally made my way to the vet. The appointment had been made earlier for his date with destiny, and I left him in the car to check in. When I went back out the door to fetch him, there he sat, strong and upright in the passenger seat, knowing what was coming by the look on his face. His eyes were bright and smiling as if to say, "I know."

What followed was nothing short of heart-wrenching for me as they put my big dog up on the shiny metal table and steadied his foreleg for the injection that would bring permanent sleep. I held his head in both my hands, kissed the spot between his eyes, and rubbed his favorite spot by the slope of his nose. One breath later, he was gone. There I was, a six-foot-two, two-hundred-pound, sobbing mass of sadness. I am not ashamed to inform you that, as I recount and write this chapter, tears are streaming down my face as if all of this happened just moments ago. I suppose, in the grand scheme of things, they have.

I was inconsolable for days, and the mere sight of his leash or collar would send me into deep sadness. And then, about a week later, I picked up Jake's ashes and headed out to the woods to deposit a little bit of him there. I knelt at one of his favorite trees, carved out a small hole in the ground, and began to pour the ash into my hand and then into the ground. That is when the moment caught me. While Jake's physical presence was missed deeply, I realized that what I had really lost was who I was when he was with me. It was the sense of companionship, the unconditional love, the fun, and the adventure; sleeping in the back of the truck, wading through rivers, camping in Florida, and watching in wonder as he slept at my feet; just the two of us, living side by side. It was the true meaning of friendship, one of us giving commands and the other commanding me with his look, his giving of a paw, or licking my hands. It was give and take, back and forth. Perfect balance.

If you look on the middle shelf of a bookcase in the lower level of my house, nestled between an Olympia Beer stein, an autographed football, and a knife given to me by my grandfather, you'll find a white cylinder about the size of a soda can. On the top is a simple inscription: "Jake . . . November 2, 1992." Inside, of course, are the remains of the big dog with whom I have yet to part. Sixteen years have come and gone since that day I took him to the vet, but while the white color of the urn has faded with time, the lessons Jake gave me have not. If I could be half the man that he saw me as—loving, providing, and giving—then our time together would never end. Jake . . . greeting me with love and joy, no matter how my day went . . . being farmed out to others and returning with only thanks . . . missing me so much that he would howl for me in the night. Our four-legged companions seem to be masters and examples of the most powerful force in the universe—love—the one thing that humans long for and, so often, cannot find.

Man is dog's ideal of what God should be.
—HOLBROOK JACKSON (1874–1948)

2

Boomerang

Say the word "boomerang," and the first thing that comes to mind is the aboriginal people of Australia using these flying wood weapons for hunting and the like. While not all boomerangs are designed to make the return trip, the ones that are created to be thrown away and come back as if on demand are really a marvel of technology, especially when you consider that some early humans figured out how to carve a piece of wood that would act as an airfoil with enough lift to ensure that it returned to its owner. Life often serves up opportunities to carve a moment out of time and throw it into the wind, only to have it return to you in a most amazing way.

I have never been very comfortable in the Big Apple, and I am sure that two factors contribute to my discontent. First, the whole "Cubs lose pennant to Mets in '69" thing, and second, I am sure that the next cab ride I take will be my last—with the likes of Travis Bickle, Robert DeNiro's mentally unstable character from *Taxi Driver,* behind the wheel. That's not to say that I have not had some, well . . . *one* really good cabbie not attempt to set a land speed record from LaGuardia to mid-town Manhattan. I know that time is money, and far be it for me to keep a man from his good coin, but if I wanted to take a thrill ride, I would be in line at Six Flags for the Viper. With all that said, my work takes me to New York quite often, and I do my best to keep a low profile, mingle with the locals, and not tip off anyone that I think Chicago is a superior city in every way except in baseball.

With the average train trip from Chicago to New York taking just about seventeen hours, the preferred mode of transportation would be the two-hour flight from O'Hare to LaGuardia, but then, as previously mentioned, the cab ride to the city is a whole other trip in itself. However, through the generosity of my employer (and a threat to never, ever go back to New York without a car to and from the airport), a nice, retired gentleman wearing a black suit and sporting neatly combed hair smelling slightly of Old Spice is standing by the down escalator with a sign that reads "St. Augustine." It's not quite as compelling as I have made it sound here, but it is nice to know that someone is waiting for you who has, in fact, passed a driver's test, and there's a good chance he is not on parole at the present time. I have run into some real characters and learned some things that I am sure will come into play at some point in my life—or maybe not.

I usually take the first flight to New York and stay for three or four days. Of course, that means a return trip to Chicago that I usually take at night. I really enjoy seeing the skyline all lit up when I cross Lake Michigan on our descent into the Windy City. However, if you have been reading the papers lately, air travel has been getting, well, let's say a little "off the mark" when it comes to departures and arrivals actually taking off and landing on time. This factor contributes to a few schedule changes now and then, and even seasoned travelers get down to their last nerve when having to be rerouted and the like. I do my best to be Zenlike when commercial airline chaos ensues and to see all things as part of the giant cosmic puzzle, but when that doesn't work I do the human thing and get ticked off. Then something usually comes along to humble me one more time and show how moments really matter.

As I recall, it had been a long day, and for reasons that are vague now, I would be lucky to get back in my Chicago digs before midnight. There had been some weather delays, and after a marathon stint in the friendly confines of LaGuardia, I was able to get the last seat on the last flight home. It was a smaller jet, but as long as the wings were working and the tank was full, it looked like the perfect ride. I made my way to the seat assigned, just past the first-class bulkhead, stowed my bag overhead, and wedged my way into the aisle seat. Sitting next to me was a young woman with intense dark eyes that seemed less than certain about our guaranteed arrival just ninety minutes later. Her nervousness was self-evident as she sat bracing for takeoff, and we had not yet even begun to move from the gate. I thought it best to strike up a conversation to ease the tension. Her name was Vanessa.

We started to talk about her reason for being in New York, and it seems that she was connecting through from somewhere else and had also been traveling the better part of the day. There were many changes in her life, with her boyfriend and family and trying to make her way in the world, and before we knew it the plane had lifted off and headed toward Chicago. Somewhere over the northern part of the nation, the talk turned to things of a more cultural and then spiritual nature, and she announced to me that she was a Muslim.

I admitted that I didn't think I had ever actually known someone who was a Muslim, and we began to dig deeper into the pros and cons of every faith—where the line is between religion and spirituality, how each of us makes our own brand of religion fit our needs, be it declaring a jihad or declaring war. I was impressed by this twenty-something who was willing to engage in such a spirited conversation about her life and beliefs, and it was refreshing to think that not every young woman thought that hooking up with the right guy or winning some reality-show contest was the best path to tomorrow. At one point, the conversation turned to personal responsibility, away from the divine toward the individual, and what it might take to motivate or inspire one to change from who they are to who they would like to be. She declared that the writings of Dr. Wayne Dyer had been an influence on her in a very positive way, and it was another thing we had in common. Seizing the moment, I got up and dug out a copy of my first book, *Living an Uncommon Life,* which featured a chapter on Wayne, whom I had known from my talk-radio show and had become friends with over the years. When Vanessa saw my face on the book cover, she started to become a little uneasy, as if she had been talking about the down side of drinking milk only to find out she was sitting next to the milkman without knowing it.

"I didn't know you were this guru or something," she said.

"That's because I'm not," I replied. "I am searching, just as you are. I might have a few more seasons of searching under my belt, but I am still looking for more of me every chance I get."

So we got back to Wayne and his lessons on life, as well as those of a few of the other people profiled in the book. Just as time has a habit of doing when engaged in meaningful conversation, it slipped by, and it was nearly time to touch down in Chicago, with the glimmering lights of the Second City in the distance. I signed the book for Vanessa and thanked her for making the end of my day so enjoyable and reflective. She was very appreciative of the conversation and the book, and when I learned how far she still had to go to get home—a train ride to not one of the best parts of the city to wait for an aunt to pick her up—I offered to drive her home from a purely parental perspective. I have a daughter not much younger than she, and while she at first hesitated with the hour being so late, she finally agreed.

After we touched down, I got my car out of the lot, drove to the agreed-upon pickup point, and waited. After about fifteen minutes, I realized that she was not coming, but still drove around the airport for nearly an hour. My biggest concern was that she got home safely, but after thinking it over it dawned on me that maybe getting home safely was her concern as well, and taking a ride from a near stranger was the cause of that concern. I tend to still see the world as a safe place, even with all the chaos, and make every effort to keep that vision when it comes to situations like this. But I understood and probably would have chided my daughter if she had accepted a ride in a similar situation. As I drove wearily back to my apartment, I decided that what was most important had been the flight from New York, Vanessa's view of the world, and the opportunity to connect with someone so different from me in many ways—and yet so very much the same. Within a week or so, I had all but forgotten about the event.

A few months passed, and life got busy again. I had an occasional thought about Vanessa when the suburb she lived in was mentioned on the news or something, but I had other things to think about—like getting ready to face the fact that I was almost fifty. The qualifying factor in this equation was the arrival of the dreaded high-school reunion invitation proclaiming that thirty years had evaporated right before my eyes. While I mostly felt the same inside as I did in 1977, the outer shell had, of course, changed a bit. Time had slipped by so fast that it seemed like just yesterday when we got the news that Elvis had died—or at least moved on to Fish Nose, Idaho, to sell burgers undercover. I have only stayed in touch with a handful of my classmates, many of whom I have known since grade school. Wow, talk about going back in time forty years . . . sheesh.

Reunions are a funny thing because high school is a funny thing. It's supposed to prepare you somewhat for real life, and yet very little about high school is real. I have attended all three of my reunions and have observed the following. The ten-year reunion is like still being in school. You're twenty-eight or so and still looking pretty good for the most part. You don't sit back and relive too many old memories because, frankly, they aren't that old yet, and neither are you. Then the twenty-year deal rolls around, and you are a little more apprehensive about attending because more of your chest has become part of your stomach, no matter what your gender. Some of the memories are getting a little fuzzy, and you're not sure if you have the facts right. Now, at thirty-eight, time is starting to catch up with you a little bit, and you are not sure if you want the rest of your class to see what the wear and tear of marriage, kids, mortgages, and money have etched into your brow. Then along comes the big 3-0 reunion, and by then your hide has toughened to the point of self-acceptance—been there, done that, and bought the bumper sticker. "Go ahead and honk—I couldn't care less" is the cry of the day. You've lost all the hair you're going to lose, dealt with life head-on, and lived to tell the tale. You go to the deal really ready to shake it loose, see some old friends, make some new ones, talk about the people who didn't show, and make an ass of yourself—all in the name of getting back together after three decades.

So I was feeling pretty good about myself as I went off in search of yesterday. At forty-eight, I still work out three or four times a week, have done pretty well in the career category, and have more hair than most of the guys who gave me a hard time at the twenty-year reunion. There was something special in the air that night that I could not quite get my arms around, but I wrote it off to the anticipation of reconnection . . . for better or for worse. I found parking, took a deep breath, and went inside.

There was a long table with name badges, stuck with our graduation pictures just for laughs. I had not looked at the photo for many years. I remembered that back then, they took one picture and that was it, unlike the *Teen Vogue* full-color layouts that cost as much as my first car that today's seniors insist upon. I stuck the label on my chest, went in search of something wet to drink, and ran into a pile of my old buddies who really got the ball rolling. It wasn't long before the stories came out and the laughter went up, in particular from my friend Tim, who has had me dialed in ever since fifth grade. We moved like a mob from one end of the room to the other, gathering up more and more people and more and more stories. I was amazed at how much everyone who attended was really cutting loose, and at one point, I just stood with my back against the wall and closed my eyes to listen to the laughter. It was a pretty magical thing. By the time dinner was being served, we had gathered up a fair number of our eighth-grade partners and were close to seceding from the union to form our own party and state. Oh, yeah, it was an open bar, but I don't think that really had anything to do with it.

Someone asked me if I had been to the restroom recently. Not knowing if they knew something I did not, I replied, "Maybe." "Well, then, you must have seen the picture of you in there. Matter of fact, there is one in the ladies' room, as well." Shuddering to think of what pictures, real or concocted, one of my "buddies" might have hung up in the john, I made my way in. Sure enough, taped right above the hand dryer was a copy of the *Living an Uncommon Life* book cover with my mug on it. By this point in the festivities, it was still hanging on the wall, but a few of my "friends" had added some comments and other, umm, interesting graffiti. I figured that since it was my image, I would add a couple of drawings, too, but thought it best to leave before I was caught defacing my own billboard. I was all ready to get back into the bash full swing and was making my way across the foyer to the ballroom entrance when a man stepped out from a corner and grabbed my arm. He said, "Oh, my God . . . you're John!"

My mind raced back to find some recollection of his face. He was not wearing a name tag, so I was drawing a blank. "You are the man who wrote the book that changed my life!" he continued. I was still more than a little murky on who this man might be. "I saw your face in the bathroom and wondered if you were here. It's a miracle. Honey, look, it's John!" Just then, a beautiful Hispanic woman with long hair turned away from the coat-room check-in and rushed over to hug me. What was this all about?

"A few months ago, you were on a plane from New York and sat next to my daughter, Vanessa. You signed your book to her. She told us about meeting you and gave the book to David to read. It's had a great effect on his and my life."

David stood next to me, grinning from ear to ear. However, I had to sit down because once again, I was in awe of the incredible power that makes this all happen.

What are the odds that a girl I met on a plane months earlier, after being bumped twice from other flights, would end up being the daughter of someone I went to school with thirty years earlier, in a city the size of Chicago and a graduation class of hundreds?

Talk about a reunion. Even though the hour was late, David called Vanessa. She had been awakened from a sound sleep and was in tears on the other end of the phone, which served to put some raindrops in my eyes. Vanessa apologized for not meeting me after the flight and admitted she was leery of taking a ride with a total stranger, no matter how nice I had been. I understood and was just glad that she had made it home safely. In an instant, the concept of "reunion" took on a whole new meaning. I clearly remember thinking that while my mind holds a lot of facts, figures, and mostly useless trivia, the bigger concepts of life—how it really works and even *why* it works—are a major challenge to wrap the human mind around. When these types of events occur, I always run down the list; the one that starts with, "I could have never planned this out, but if I did, what had to happen in order to pull it off?" A million little moves had to be made and followed by all involved. Even the smart-ass friend of mine who decided to make copies of my book cover and paste them in the bathrooms was part of the unfolding moment.

Not too long ago, I received a beautiful card from Lydia, thanking me for the conversation on the plane with her daughter and for writing a book that was so helpful to David. She included a couple of pictures from the reunion, one with her, David, and me huddled in the foyer, and then another with the two of us. Once again, my mind asked, "What did you learn?" There were numerous small lessons involved, such as accepting someone who is from a totally different background from mine, caring for the safety of another person's child, or even realizing that the book I wrote for myself had touched someone else, further proving that at our most basic self, we are all pretty much the same, even though we hate to admit it.

I thought for a long time about the meaning of all that had occurred and then decided that it was too early for the verdict to be read on this one. After all, it had taken thirty years for this to reveal itself to all involved, at just the right time and place—a moment that I could neither have created nor implemented on my own.

There is no such thing as chance; and what seem to us merest accident springs from the deepest source of destiny.
—FRIEDRICH SCHILLER (1759–1805)

3

Caller on Line 3

We connect with each other in a multitude of ways. A hundred and fifty years ago, you met your neighbor at the common fence that connected your property or spent the evening at the local pub catching up on news of the day. As we moved forward, radio became a force, bringing new voices into our lives, along with entertainment. That was followed, of course, by the television set, which launched images into our minds from around the nation and, eventually, the world.

Then technology became king (and queen). Today, if you don't have some form of handheld device that delivers your e-mail and makes a call for you while checking the status of your flight as you watch last night's recorded reality show, then you are behind the times. While we are getting more connected through the gadgets of the "Tech Age," I am not sure that we are creating enough "real" moments to lead to connections between us as a species. Connecting is critical for humans, and as we become ever more connected to each other through devices, it's also important to remember the greater connection we have. It's often unseen, unexplainable, and quite incredible, much more so, in my mind, than a small piece of metal that fits in your pocket and tells you everything you already know.

I was headed back north on a journey for my life. Notice I said "for" and not "of" my life because, back in 1996, I was walking "for" something, and it turned out to be for me, in so many ways. It was late October, and the wind was getting that early winter snap to it as I trudged along the road just south of the town of Whitewater, Wisconsin, where I would spend the night. My mind was filled with all of the events of the past six months or so, when my life had become undone due to circumstances—some of which I had created and others beyond my control. That combination had culminated in me and my family living in a small motel in Upper Michigan and me on this walk to find out who I was and what in heaven's name I was supposed to be doing with this life.

Walking might just be the most spiritual thing you can do when it comes to seeking clarity. Once the body is engaged and gets about its business of moving you forward, the mind somehow disengages from its bounds and is allowed to soar as it was designed to do. All manner of answers and inspiration can come your way. When I walked from Upper Michigan to Chicago and back, I followed a zigzag pattern that added many miles to the trip, but also added some fantastic scenery and incredible images that are forever etched into my mind.

This particular day, I was looking forward to reaching town, having a really hot shower, and getting some sleep in a bed. Many times on the walk, I would just drift off the road and find a stand of pine trees, pile up the needles, and nestle in for a nap; so after a while, a real pillow was a treat. As I walked north on the southbound lane, facing oncoming traffic, I passed a small gift store on my left and had the overwhelming urge to go inside. I fought the feeling for about thirty paces, not wanting to get knocked off course, but I eventually succumbed to the thought. I marched back to the little store and went inside. It was filled with all sorts of tourist trappings, but had a fair share of what looked to be real Native American items that caught my eye. As reminders of my quest, I had been carrying a few things given to me by friends on the walk, including a hand-carved pipe and assorted stones, feathers, and tobacco.

I made my way around the store, and at one point I caught a glimpse of myself in a mirror and almost did not recognize who I had become. I had lost a lot of weight as a byproduct of walking so much, subsisting mainly on nuts and a ton of water, and the beard on my face came right out of some mountain-man novel. I looked like a weary tramp, searching for a corner to put his bedroll. Despite my appearance, I connected with the people who owned the shop, and for quite some time, we talked about life and all that goes with it. I was able to offer some "road wisdom" for a few of the challenges that had come up in their lives, and as I thanked them and got ready to resume my walk, the daughter, Sheryl, offered a ride up to Whitewater, which I readily accepted. As we headed to her car, she said, "There is something I want to show you, and I am not sure why." A short way down the highway, she made a left turn and went down a small dirt road that opened up to a beautiful lake that was shimmering with the last sun of the day. On the far shore were some big homes, but to our right, a couple of small cabins stood framing the near shoreline. It was a nice way to end the day, and the lake gave me a good feeling.

"This is a good spot. Thanks for showing me this place. What's the name of this lake?" I asked. Sheryl answered, "It's called Lake Wandewaga." I froze right where I stood. The last time I had been at this lake was in the late 1960s for a weekend with my family and cousin. The church my cousin Rich attended owned a cabin on the lake, and I could clearly remember fishing from the dock at night and my mother doing a major spider-check under the sheets. Prior to Cheryl saying "Lake Wandewaga," I'd had no conscious memory of it for the past forty years and had zero idea where it was located. While it was a *Twilight Zone* moment for me, it was just one of many I had walking my way to a new life.

After much conversation, Sheryl dropped me off in the early evening just outside Whitewater, and I proceeded on to my stopover for the night. I felt humbled that whatever had drawn me so strongly to go back and talk with the people at the gift store had also led me to a spot that, while not sacred, was surely special in my life. A few years later, the memory of that event stayed with me, but the people with whom I had talked became another silhouette on the backdrop of this trek. As time went on, I forgot just about everything from that stop except the image of the lake.

Fast-forward ten years to 2006. My life had changed dramatically since the walk ended a decade earlier. Many of the visions I'd had while walking had come to pass. I had created and hosted a very successful talk-radio show, authored a book that was soon to come out, and was about to move on to satellite radio. It was with all this in tow that I was invited to be a guest on the *Ben Merens Show* on Wisconsin Public Radio to talk about the journey that each of us is on and perhaps provide some guideposts to look for when exploring a life. Along with me on the air was my close friend and walking partner, Duane Kinnart.

Before I move on with this story, I am compelled to acknowledge the "higher voices" in radio, be it public, AM/FM, or satellite. It does not take much talent or preparation to simply find that which is not working in the world and pound it into people's lives on a daily basis, further stifling the human spirit. It does, however, take talent and preparation to look for that which *is* working in the world and bring it forth to *nurture* the human spirit. My hat is off and microphone on to those deeply dedicated voices who bring out the best in each of us. They understand that radio is more than just selling airtime or a maze of wire and cable.

It's about intention and vibration. And if we raise both of them, then anyone within earshot is reminded that life is about choices and chances, not just rants and raves. There are far too many voices on the air that talk as if they know everything about everything but haven't done much of anything.

So, to continue with my story: we were sitting high above the city of Milwaukee talking with Ben (who is the consummate radio pro and one who does challenge his listeners) about the walk, what lessons we had learned, and how each of us has a walk to take, if not in the physical then surely in the spiritual. About halfway though the show, Ben announced that there was a caller on line 3 who had met me on the walk in 1996. My mind was racing to see who this could be because nothing stood out.

Jane came on the line and told our listeners, "We met John when we owned a small gift store near Whitewater. He was walking north and stopped in for a while. He bought a couple of gifts for his family that I shipped for him, and he came at just the right time. We were uncertain about a lot of things in our life at that time, and John's words gave us hope and direction. My daughter Sheryl gave him a ride to town and stopped on the way at a small lake that she said had a tremendous effect on him. They talked about the journey of life, and he gave her a few small sunflower seeds. He said that each of us has the seed of possibility within, and it's our job to make sure we nurture it so it blossoms. Not a day has gone by in the past ten years that we haven't thought about and prayed for John, not knowing if he made it home or what became of him. Then today, my son was listening to Ben's show, and he called me and yelled into the phone, 'Mom, it's John!' So I tried a few times and finally got through, and I just wanted to thank John for what he said to us so many years ago and what a blessing he has been for our family."

After hearing Jane's words, you could have scraped up what was left of me and put it in a test tube. My ears could not believe what they were hearing. This woman and her family had remembered my name, where I lived, what I had bought as a gift, and had prayed for me for the past ten years. I was reduced to tears and barely had enough in me to respond to her. Wisely, Ben went to break, and I spoke to Jane off the air and made arrangements to meet. Duane had to do most of the talking in the second half of the show because my train of thought had been derailed big time. I was overwhelmed at the concept of perfect strangers giving any consideration to me in any way, shape, or form past a short stop for less than an hour ten years before.

Duane and I, along with our friend Doug and his son Sam, headed to Chicago a few weeks later for a weekend gathering and decided that we would call Jane on the way back north. We did just that and then proceeded to the small town in Wisconsin to which they had relocated. The trip had been incredible up to that point, and it became even more of a gift when I saw Sheryl standing in front of her parents' apartment wearing a bright pink sweater. We hugged and introduced each other and hugged some more. As we walked down the hallway to the apartment, Duane suddenly grabbed my arm. "Did you see what's on that door?" I spun around and walked a couple of doors back. On the front door of an apartment was a picture of singer/songwriter John Denver and the words to part of a song called "Looking for Space":*

> On the road of experience, trying to find my own way,
> sometimes I wish that I could fly away.
> When I think that I am moving, suddenly things stand still,
> and I'm afraid 'cause I think they always will.
> And I'm looking for space and to find out who I am,
> and I'm looking to know and understand.

*From the album *Windsong*. ©1975 by Cherry Lane Music. Used by permission.

It wasn't the usual thing you see on a front door, and the fact that Mr. Denver was a friend and mentor to me added to the moment. Something was going on . . . I could feel it in my bones. We finally entered the apartment along with Sheryl to meet Jane and Tom and their son and daughter-in-law. The rooms were filled with the same Native American artifacts and etchings that I had seen ten years earlier, and a beautiful wolf dog sat right at Tom's feet. We caught up on years of stories, laughter, and tears, and at one point we stood in a circle and just listened to each other breathe. I was compelled to give Tom my father's college ring to wear as he battled cancer, and other gifts were exchanged. It was an incredible reunion that had been years in the making. There were so many amazing events that had been a part of each life that it took much time to share them all. As night grew near and the long ride ahead beckoned, we said our reluctant good-byes and headed north.

Doug, Duane, and I talked for nearly the entire four hours home about the many and varied ways in which the universe seems to line up everything in perfect form—if we get out of the way. Even those events that seem small and meaningless might turn out to be big and meaningful as the years roll by. The entire weekend was without any real plan, which allowed the bigger plan to play itself out. We felt a bit like chess pieces that had been moved on the board of life to be in the right place at the right time to set in motion more magical moments.

A couple of years have passed since the reach of radio brought a group of people back together, and I still stay in touch with Jane and Tom, and call when I am passing through the area. We catch up on things and, of course, always remark how "remarkable" were the circumstances that had to be arranged for all of us to meet and for reasons that are still revealing themselves.

What is it that speaks to us and says, "go back" or "turn left"? I suppose it has many names—intuition, the inner voice or guide—but those are just human terms for something that seems to be more "being" than "human," and also seems to get easier to hear the more connected we become to the inner world. For me, it was on a walk, but it has also happened while I am driving or very tired, when my resistance to inner instruction is low. Strangely, this inner guide always has our best interests in "mind," for lack of a better term. Here is what I know about this force or guidance: When I listen to it, *really* listen and get it, then all manner of events fall together in perfect harmony and cadence. The time that it takes becomes irrelevant because that still, small voice seems not to operate on the man-made time zones we are all used to. Even with all the evidence presented here and scores of other times when that which is within beckons me, I still sometimes balk when the unseen mentor suggests a course of action or change in my life. It's a tough gig, this human thing, but the "being" part of me delights in watching me grow.

> *Let your heart be your guide on all things,*
> *but you have to listen closely because it speaks so softly.*
> —JOHN ST. AUGUSTINE

— 4 —

Captain Dracula

In the picture, he looks like most young men who grew up in the early 1950s, with a square jaw and horn-rimmed glasses. His hair is short on the sides and long on the top, held in place by a substantial amount of "butch wax," I would guess. The tie has some weird pattern on it, but the collars of his shirt are sharp and crisp, a tribute to my grandmother's prowess with an iron and spray starch. There are no worry lines across his face or trace of the beard he wore most of his life—just a broad smile that seemed to go from ear to ear. When this photo was taken, he had not yet met my mother, and neither I nor my sister Laurie were even a thought in his young mind. Most of his life was in front of him. A college scholarship awaited—he wanted to be an architect— and what I am struck by most in this picture of my dad are his eyes. They are focused on some far-off direction as if looking into his future and wondering what life holds in store for him. One of the most important moments in my life is when those eyes closed for the last time.

My father was waiting for me so he could die. The last thing I wanted to do was go see him because I knew that once the cycle was set in motion, there would be no turning back. Even though we did not always see eye to eye, the death of my father would mean, among other things, that I had moved to the head of the line, a place that no little boy inside every man is ever ready for.

On a Thursday night, I went to sleep and had an amazing dream. I was walking up the stairs to my old family home, and I entered the main hallway that was as I remember it—a floor-to-ceiling bookcase on my right and a staircase that led up to the second floor on my left. When I came to the end of that hallway, I turned around and began to walk out again. As I did, the entire house began to turn to gold. When I reached the front porch, my father stood there in his pajamas, looking very small and sickly. With arms stretched out to me, he said, "Butch, I want to go home." I picked him up—he was light as a feather—and he kissed my cheek, smiled, and said, "Let's go!" I knew that it was a sign for me to let go of my fear and take my place in the last chapter of his life.

The next morning, I told Jackie about the dream, threw a few things in a suitcase, and headed south. As I drove to Chicago from Michigan on my way to the hospital, I had nearly six hours to think about the man, the lessons he had taught me, and the moments that had changed me, most without my ever knowing it.

Dad grew up in Chicago and had set his sights on college and a career in architecture when his parents' divorce put a wrench in the plans. Just a few hours shy of his college degree, he quit school and went to work to help his mom pay the bills. Years later, it would be one of the biggest regrets of his life—not going back to finish what he had started—and it was a pattern that followed him most of his life. He took a job working in a savings and loan operation and quickly moved up to a supervisory position. Thus, the golden handcuffs were clamped in place. The college dreams slowly faded into a drawer marked "Later," and he went about making a life for himself on another track.

Somewhere along the line, he met a blonde-haired, blue-eyed young woman named Carol Benson and fell in love. In September 1957, they were married. He had just turned twenty-one, and Carol was only twenty. In December 1958, I arrived on the planet two days before the New Year, just in time to help with the tax return. Two years later, just about the same time the Soviets launched *Venera 1* toward the planet Venus, my sister came on board. I have always thought that she was somehow a byproduct of space experimentation.

As I drove south, fragments of my early life tumbled toward me like so many puzzle pieces . . . a brick two-story flat on a street whose name escapes me . . . living upstairs from my grandmother on Fletcher Avenue, within walking distance of the famed Riverview Amusement Park in the early 1960s . . . watching the fireworks from the park light up the Chicago River that flowed next to the Material Service Corporation, a gravel yard that had elephant-sized cement trucks coming and going (usually over the curb by the house, a maneuver that sent my grandmother into fits).

We moved from my grandma's house (a move that devastated me at the age of eight because it meant leaving my best friend Gary and all the wonders of that house . . . the coal-burning furnace that had to be fed at all hours of the night . . . the attic that was filled with relics and rubbish . . . the baseball diamond at the end of the alley so brilliantly disguised by adults as a lumber yard) to a big old Victorian on Berteau Avenue that would be the family home for the next thirty-five years. That house became my dad's castle (in more ways than one), and the moments created there are never far away from my mind.

If you lived on the northwest side of Chicago from 1968 to 1979 and stood in line with a few hundred other kids in the last days before Halloween, chances are you have been in the basement (or should I say "haunted" basement) of our home. The ritual started back when my dad was a kid, building spooky houses with his buddies, and he carried it forward to his adult years.

The activity usually started in late August or early September when the plans were drawn up for the maze, monsters, and mayhem that would be unleashed in the lower level. The basement was cleaned out, and cardboard walls were built that would house a most gruesome lineup: The Wolfman (my cousin Rich), Frankenstein's Monster (Uncle Ken, and sometimes Mr. Stich from across the street), and, of course, Dr. Frankenstein (a rotating cast of my dad's buddies), and some guy with a circular saw that seemed to cut his leg off. (This came in the later years after the slasher-type movies became popular.) And, finally, there was the Prince of Darkness himself, Count Dracula . . . the guy I called Dad. Christopher Lee would have been proud of his get-up, complete with handmade cape by Mrs. Dracula (my mother) from some heavy drapes that once hung in my room, slicked-back widow's peak hairdo, bone-white face makeup, and fangs that he kept in a small glass box in his sock drawer when not in use. Around his neck hung a heavy, metal German-looking cross, something he bought at the county fair on a vacation to Appleton. (Yes, it was a bit out of character for Dracula to be wearing anything with an intersection, but somehow this thing seemed okay.)

One look from the old man in the basement in full garb gently lit by the glow of the red bulb stuck inside the plastic skull, and young and old alike huddled together like sheep, bleating and screaming their way through the maze and past monsters until they made it upstairs into our kitchen and out the front door. Hundreds of people signed the "ghost book" over the years, and it gave my dad great delight to not only scare the shit out of people, but also for a few nights a year to go from banker to Bela Lugosi, to escape from the routine and use his creative energy in a way that made people happy. Halloween and the week prior were the happiest times of my dad's life.

As I drew closer to Chicago, I called my sister and checked on his condition. Things were going from bad to worse, and he was in and out of reality. At one point, he told her that the crew from the *Starship Enterprise* had beamed into his room and demanded that he go with them, but only after getting the answer to a question . . . an answer he was sure that I was bringing him. How would I deal with this turn of events? I was having a hard enough time thinking about what life would be like without him, and now I was supposed to provide the answer to some unknown question that would allow him to cross over into the next galaxy and boldly go where he had never gone before.

While my dad never attended a *Star Trek* convention or dressed up like Mr. Spock, he was hooked on the short-lived TV show that now lives forever in reruns. Growing up in the fifties, my dad was like a lot of the kids in America—immersed in anything to do with space travel or beings from another planet. It was the birth of sci-fi as we know it, and so much of what seemed like schlock and camp on the screen has shown up in our daily lives. Captain Kirk's communicator looks strangely like my cellphone, and the little PDA that attaches to my hip and buzzes when someone thinks they need me could have been worn on the belt by any self-respecting Klingon. More often than not, you could find my dad after work, with TV table in place, perched on the corner of the couch watching Kirk, Spock, Bones, Scotty, and Sulu keep the universe in order as only they could. It was just another way for him to forget about customers and the accounts that were overdue at the bank and knock off a few aliens in frustration.

As I made my way into the heart of Chicago, the more all the memories of my mom (who passed away in 1997) and dad swirled around in my head. As I sat in the street traffic, I thought about a conversation about life, lessons, and love that I'd had with my dad not too many months before he got really sick.

For years, my dad would thaw frozen pipes in the basement with a hot blowdryer. The winter of 1999 brought about the same ritual, but this time there would be unusual consequences. My mom had died a couple of winters earlier, and to this day when I think about him wandering around the house without her, my spirit sags. I dedicated my first book to them—"To John and Carol, sweethearts then *and* now"—in tribute to the fact that while both of them battled their way through life on their own terms, the love between them and how much my father adored my mother, through thick and thin, was evident for all to see. Keeping the house warm was Dad's job.

So the innovator turned on the blowdryer and began to thaw the cold steel when the telephone rang in the basement. He propped up the device in the slats of the wall and answered the phone. As he got ready to hang up, the front doorbell rang, so he got off the horn, went upstairs, and opened the door. A nice gentleman asked my dad if he knew that his house was on fire. My dad stepped out into the icy alley next to the house and saw five-foot-high flames shooting out of the roof! It seems that the old newspaper that had been wrapped around the pipes finally caught a spark after all these years. He rushed back to the basement, turned off the blowdryer and tried to put out the blaze with handfuls of snow from the backyard. By then, however, the fire was in the walls. Eventually, Engine 69 showed up and put out the blaze, but the fire and water damage were too much to live with—literally. The house was not a total loss, but it's tough to sleep in the master bedroom with a hole in the roof.

Dad moved in with my sister and that worked for a little while, but he was like a caged lion. He was used to roaming his castle as lord of the manor and now he spent too much time in a lounge chair in the corner, surrounded by grandkids he loved dearly but was not used to being around all the time. As my sister was nearing the end of a divorce, they decided to put the old house up for sale as is, hope some rehabber would buy it, and purchase a house that would give her and the kids a place and him much more room to move around. Eventually, they did find a home with enough space for all of them and a garage for his latest unfinished project—a 1966 Mustang convertible.

Putting the house up for sale was really difficult. He had envisioned restoring the house to its original 1890s condition, even to the point of using his long-ignored architecture background to draw up plans. He was deeply connected to that home, and in some strange way the fire was a signal of things to come for him, purging his past and making way for the final chapter of his life. A few months after they moved into the new place, a rehab guy did appear on the scene, details were worked out, and he began to slowly put the old place together. A year or so later, it looked much as it had in the late 1800s, with a few upgrades, of course.

I visited Dad in Chicago as time would allow—in between trying to build my radio career and make sure the kids kept shoes on their feet. I had taken a much-needed but very difficult hiatus from radio that was way longer than I had expected. It did, however, afford me time to spend with my dad. One particular night flashed through my mind as I rounded the last corner to the hospital.

My dad had taken to sleeping in his lounge chair for much of the night, and the pull-out couch, where I slept when I visited, was in the living room as well. Dad would watch television until very late, then go up to bed and come down again in time to plop in the chair and wait for the clock radio to wake him around five or so in the morning. As I drifted off to sleep, not remembering the last time I had slept in the same room as my father (around the age of four maybe?), he suddenly spoke in the darkness. "I am really glad that you are here tonight." I lay there, not knowing how or if I should answer. *Maybe I should pretend to be asleep . . . like a four-year-old.* Instead, I simply said, "I'm glad, too, Dad." That one short reply set off a three-hour-plus conversation that had been years in the making. Sometimes the words were hard, and sometimes they were heartfelt, but all of them needed to be said. And as he sat in the chair illuminated by the giant-screen television, and I lay in the bed talking about our lives as father and son, the gap between us melted away as if it had never been there.

That late-night talk shed new light on my dad (and it wasn't just the blue hue of the sixty-inch plasma that was getting a bit creepy). At one point, the conversation turned to careers and earning a living. My dad freely confessed that his parents' divorce affected him on levels that still made themselves known in his life. He looked back on a series of projects that all went unfinished, mostly around the house, that directly tied back to his not completing his one big goal—to graduate from college. This had manifested over the years as closets with no doors, paneling with no edges, and assorted other "almost done" events. Like most of us, he put his dreams on hold when love, kids, and bills came knocking. He talked about unfulfilled goals and wondering each morning when he readied to go off to work how his life might have been different if a college degree had been hanging on the wall. My dad did pretty well without the paper, but for him it was something that meant a great deal. As the years rolled on, the unfinished business became a "woulda, coulda, shoulda" trifecta that never paid off. I suddenly did not see him as my father. His words gave me the image of a young man who was full of hope and ideas, but circumstances seemingly beyond his control had derailed him, and he never fully recovered. Somehow, the unfinished closet in my room didn't seem to matter anymore.

I told him of my vivid memory of watching him get ready to go to work in the morning—the routine of shaving and "brushing his fangs," slapping on some Hai Karate, and leaving for the bank at the same time every day. He would walk the two miles or so to work and sometimes would walk home for lunch. But what stayed with me most was seeing him round the corner by the Connors' house and come striding toward our front yard after a full day. While the pace was brisk, there was often a look on his face that told another story. While he was fulfilling his role as father and provider, he went unfulfilled on the inside, going back and forth to a job that he "had" to do. It was that knowing I had as a kid that propelled me to seek not just a job but a *calling*, to refuse to let circumstances define me, no matter what they may be. Finishing what you start (within reason) became of vital importance.

Sitting on that couch bed somewhere around two in the morning, I told him that my success, whatever it may be, was a direct result of watching him over the years and learning the lessons previously mentioned. Having a workmanlike mentality to go day in and day out in a radio career, oftentimes with little to show but letters from listeners, gave me the discipline I needed to move forward. Suddenly, it was his turn to see the son in a different way. No longer was I wandering aimlessly down some dead-end road. I was picking up the mantle of an unfinished life and putting my own touches on it, like some great race in which the baton had passed from one generation to the next. It was my turn to see how far I could run before I had to hand off to my son Andy. Perhaps that's the real measure of success—what we attempt, not always the "things" we accomplish.

As night moved toward morning, the talk became less frequent, but by then the thoughts and words hung in the air like a string of kites . . . how much he enjoyed watching the leaves change . . . the sorrow and guilt he felt for not being able to help my mom get healthy . . . how proud he was of the grandkids . . . why he thought the best car he had ever owned was a 1970 Buick GS . . . how difficult it was for him not to spend his later and last years in the house he dearly loved . . . and how much it meant to him when we bowled together in the late-night men's league for a few years. As he talked, there were times I would fall in and out of sleep, only catching a sentence here or there, but I don't think it mattered much to him. What was most important was that what he had held on to much of his life was coming out into the light of day, even though it was pitch dark.

My thoughts returned to the present, and I found a parking space in the hospital lot. I headed to the critical-care unit and joined the family members who had been watching over him for the past week. My sister mentioned again the whole *Star Trek* thing and that she hoped I would have the answers to whatever questions Dad might have. (She wasn't the only one!) I left the waiting room, steadied myself outside the hospital room, pulled back the curtain by the door, and walked in.

He was so pale, and the eyes that I had looked into a million times were laced with fear because, on some level, he knew what was going on. I walked over to the bed, and he simply said, "'Bout time you got here." I put my hand on his forehead, which was very hot.

"Do you want me to put a cold cloth on your head?" I asked.

He answered, "Yeah, that would feel good."

I found a rag, doused it and folded it neatly, and then placed it across his head.

"So what's this I hear that Captain Kirk and the crew have been here?" I said.

Dad looked up at me and replied in a very serious tone, "They have come for me twice, and I did not know the answer to the question. You have to help me. You know the answer."

I swallowed hard. "What's the question, Dad?"

He closed his eyes and lay back on the pillow. "How do you kill the enemy inside? There are three in me. They have to be destroyed. Once I battle them and prove that I can join the crew, then I can go with Kirk and Spock."

I took a seat next to the bed and thought, *The enemy inside? Three of them? And I have the answer?* After a while, the thought came to me that my dad was fighting cancer, he'd had a kidney transplant, and his feet were a great source of pain to him, disfigured and swollen from various drugs. These three things could be called an enemy within, but how would he fight against the inevitable? He was dying, going in and out of consciousness, and I knew I'd better think fast because the last thing I wanted was to have the *Starship Enterprise* crew show up again and leave him behind. If I didn't come up with an answer, they might set their phasers on mutilate and fry my ass.

Then I thought about something my dad used to do when we would horse around in the yard. When he wanted to stop the roughhousing, he would come up and give me the feared "Vulcan Mind Melt" that our play Mr. Spock often used to demolish aliens and the like. He would place his hand on the top of my head in a clawlike manner, hum really loudly, and pronounce that he was melting my brain from the inside out. Maybe that was the answer!

"Dad, remember how Spock used his brain power to destroy aliens? He would battle them with his mind. That's how you have to fight the three enemies inside you. You can do what he did!"

My dad got this big smile on his face, looked at me with eyes now devoid of fear, and went off to battle the intruders. I watched his face closely. His eyes twitched, the small muscles on his face shuddered, and his head went back and forth. In his own mind, he was in the battle of a lifetime, and it would be something that he would make sure he finished on his terms.

I stayed in the hospital that night. Shortly after three in the morning, a huge storm woke me up. I had fallen asleep on the couch in the waiting room. Remembering where I was, I quickly went to my dad's room. He was asleep, looking just like he did in the lounge chair at home. I went back to the waiting room and flipped on the television. I couldn't believe what was on the tube . . . it was the final few moments from *Star Trek IV: The Voyage Home* where Kirk and the crew are thanking a pod of whales for helping them save the planet. I could not believe my eyes. And then, the most amazing thing, the next movie on the channel was *Dracula,* starring Christopher Lee. I sat there with my mouth hanging open, watching the storm rage outside, and the two most important pieces of the life puzzle my dad had put in place playing back-to-back on the television. What were the odds? And who was going to believe this? I sat and watched *Dracula,* occasionally checking on Dad until the movie was over and I fell back to sleep.

A nurse woke me around seven to tell me that I needed to call the family because Dad was fading fast. I phoned my sister and "Wolfman Rich" and went in to be with Dad. I held his left hand for a long time, studying it, not wanting to forget it. He still wore his wedding ring even after Mom had died, but it was loose on his finger now because of the sickness. My sister came, and the two of us stood by as the time drew nearer, moment by moment. At one point, a nurse came in and began to whisper in his ear with a thick East Indian accent. *"Go to God, John. It's okay . . . just go to God now . . . "* She touched his arm tenderly when she spoke, and it was as if she had some ancient agreement to be there when he passed. With the nurse and my sister in the room, I took a break, but no sooner had I arrived in the waiting room to call home, the nurse came in and said, "Come now." I walked back into the room just in time to see the heart-rate monitor go to a flat line. He was gone.

The early morning sun shining through a sky that had been scrubbed clean from the downpour the previous night lighted the room. He lay motionless on the bed, and every trace of pain and fear that had been etched into his face during the last years of his life was totally erased. His skin took on an almost alabaster hue, clean and flawless. My sister removed his wedding ring and put it on the necklace she wore. We cried a bit and held each other for a while, gazing at the man who had given us life, made sure we had clothes on our backs, food in our bellies, and a roof over our heads, and asked very little in return. After a time, my sister left the room to talk with the nurses, and I remained behind for a bit, not wanting to extract myself from this once-in-a-lifetime moment. One thought kept running through my head: *He was here when you were born, and you are here to see him die. Somehow it feels like it's the same thing.* To this day, I am not sure I know exactly what that means, but somehow it explains everything . . . all of it. Life and death are both our most intimate friends, which we experience totally on our own.

I placed my hand on my father's chest, thanked him for being the man that he was, kissed his forehead, and left the room. In the hall, my cousin Rich and his wife Marie were waiting. Rich went in, and I talked with Marie in the hallway. Somehow the subject of what I had seen on television a few hours before came up, and it turned out that Marie had been up at the same time and saw exactly what I did. I had a witness!

Later, my aunt and sister told me of other "events" that could be in a Stephen King movie, like my dad asking for an old-fashioned chocolate soda and knowing where to get one near the hospital, even though he had never been in the area before. When the group went to the place he told them, the woman behind the counter was eager to make a chocolate soda. They took it back to his room, where he had just a few sips, and they decided to go back to the café for lunch. When they arrived a few hours later, there was a sign on the window that said "Closed for Renovation." Upon looking in the window, the place looked like no one had been there for some time!

Word spread quickly, arrangements were made, and mourners filled the funeral home to overflowing. People whom my dad had worked with over the years recounted how much they had enjoyed working with him and how much he had talked about his family on the job. Old bowling buddies shared stories of late-night lane antics and how Dad was the one they could count on to keep everyone steady when those really tough matches came down to the last pin or two. Neighbors I had not seen in years stopped in, and we all reminisced about block parties, barbeques, late nights on the porch watching Cubs games, and, of course, Halloween. There was a lot of laughter at the wake, and every now and then I would glance at the front of the parlor and think to myself, *Death is the great equalizer—the one thing that we all have in common no matter how we vote, what we have, or who we think we are.* All the "things" my dad had accumulated over the years were packed in boxes somewhere, but the people who had crossed his path and touched his life, as he touched theirs, were the true measure of his very short sixty-nine years on Earth.

I gave the eulogy and spoke about how my dad had always joked about a Viking funeral. He wanted to be put on a boat of some sort and shipped out to sea as well-wishers threw torches at the vessel that was headed for Valhalla. I talked about what it was like to be the son of a man who would spend hours getting the basement ready for Halloween so he could scare the crap out of people—and have the time of his life doing it. As I spoke, I would glance to my left at the coffin and keep talking in the hope that I would not have to stop because that would mean the end of the service. As I was fishing around for my last few words, it was as if my dad were speaking to me directly. I said out loud, "It's important to finish what you start, but what's most important is starting . . . setting something out in front of you, just out of reach so that you stretch and grow as you move through life. My dad started college, and while he spent a lot of time thinking about not finishing over the years, I learned from him that circumstances should not dictate your life. Nothing is over until you decide that it is. Along the way, the path is going to change more than a few times, and it's best to go with the way of things and not push the river." As the last few words came out of my mouth, it dawned on me that my relationship with my dad had been perfect. Had he been different, then I would have been different, and I was getting more and more okay with who I am. It was in that moment that I totally accepted myself—faults and successes, good and bad. For better or worse, till death catches up with me. He was a perfect teacher, even though for most of my life I could not see it.

The following spring, we took my parents' ashes to a small cemetery in Wisconsin, where my mom had grown up. I dug a hole at the site of her parents' grave and carefully filled it with the remains. I covered it up, and we stood around in silence for a few minutes. The wind from the west made the field grass dance, the sun was warm on our faces, and we each took a moment to think about how short life really is.

On the days when I sit down to write, I see the picture with my father's face from more than a half-century ago. The eyes are bright and clear, looking to some far-off horizon with anticipation and hope. I smile, thinking that he finished what he started—as all of us will do someday.

A man's desire for a son is usually nothing but the wish to duplicate himself in order that such a remarkable pattern may not be lost to the world.
—HELEN ROWLAND (1875–1950)

— 5 —

Changing of the Guard

The new replacing the old is something that occurs naturally, for the most part. Summer gives way to fall with its shorter days and colder nights. Fall magically transforms into winter. Here in the Upper Peninsula of Michigan, winter is more than a season; it's like a relative who comes to visit and stays way too long. But even in the U.P., the snow eventually becomes part of the rivers and streams and makes way for spring and all its glory. And that, of course, leads to another summer. Sometimes, change goes unnoticed; other times, it's on display for all to witness.

Perhaps one of the most famous of all changes takes place in the United Kingdom, where tourists from all over the world come to watch the Changing of the Guard in the forecourt of Buckingham Palace. The St. James' Palace detachment of the Queen's Guard, usually led by the Drum Corps, marches along the Mall to Buckingham Palace, where the Buckingham Palace detachment has formed up to await its arrival. These two detachments are the Old Guard. At the very same time, the New Guard is forming up and awaits inspection by the Adjutant on the parade square. The Band, having been inspected by the Adjutant, forms a circle to play music whilst the New Guard is inspected. When the New Guard is formed up, led by the Band, it marches across into the forecourt of Buckingham Palace. Then the New

Guard marches toward the Old Guard in slow time and stops. The Old Guard presents arms, followed by the New Guard doing the same. The Captains of the Guards then march toward each other, and they exchange the Palace keys. The new reliefs are marched to the guardrooms of Buckingham Palace and St. James' Palace where new sentries are posted.

As a father *and* a son, I know exactly what it feels like to be handed those keys and then pass them on. But my relief doesn't wear a big furry hat and march in place; he just flies through the air with the greatest of ease and a basketball in his hands.

Nineteen ninety-one was quite a year. It's a palindrome (a word, sequence, or phrase that reads the same in either direction), and humans were about their usual antics. It was the year that we learned the term "scud" as it pertains to missiles. (Other "scuds" include The Scud Mountain Boys, "scud running"— an aviation term, and, of course, Canadian journalist Arthur "Scud Stud" Kent, so named for his coverage of the Gulf War.) The late leader of Iraq, Saddam Hussein, sealed his fate, so to speak, by invading Kuwait, to which twelve countries responded by pounding the dictator—if not into submission, at least into a more benign state. We all got the chance to watch "real" reality television as the bombing raids lit up the night sky over Baghdad right in our living rooms. On a much lighter note, Garth Brooks was on top of the musical heap in 1991, Fox Network rolled out condom ads on the tube (sorry), and Pee Wee Herman dropped his trousers. (How could he not, with a name like that?) On January 23 of that year, NBC launched a new show you might have heard of called *Seinfeld*. I wasn't home to watch that first famous episode because my wife and I were a little busy that day (actually, she was busier than I was)

as offspring number two arrived on planet Earth at his designated coordinates.

I knew his name was Andy long before he arrived, almost as if he were announcing his arrival in some psychic way. Andrew (as his mom calls him) is a name of Greek origin and means "man warrior." Andrew was the first chosen of the twelve apostles. (I wonder if Peter called him Andy.) St. Andrew is the patron saint of Scotland and Russia. Andy Griffith made the name a household one. All that being said, my Andy is most definitely a warrior, a man in the making (which is quite the process to watch). He may never become a patron saint, but he will sit and watch Mayberry with the old man and laugh out loud as Barney Fife does his thing. In short, Andy is the New Guard marching toward the Old Guard in slow, measured steps. It becomes more evident each day that, in many ways, he has evolved to a new level of consciousness, physical prowess, and "life awareness"— far higher than I ever had when I had reached eighteen and one I often forget at the age of fifty.

In the course of being a father, one sees the son as a mirror image of himself in so many ways, constantly on the lookout for similarities that can give us reason to exclaim, "That's my boy!" or gaps in the genetic code that allow for "He's *your* son!" Truth be told, he is not just my attempt at keeping the lineage alive, but he is a product of countless generations before me—their hopes and fears, their triumphs and their tragedies. A billion little leaves had to be placed just right on the family tree over the past few centuries for him to show up on the planet the way that he has. He has given me myriad moments that just make me glow, but it wasn't until I actually watched him fly in the air that I knew the evolutionary bar had just been raised.

A photograph of him dressed up as a Chicago Bear and standing next to his cousin John (who wears the uniform of the Kansas

City Chiefs, for some reason) started all of this. They have their arms on each other's shoulders, their helmets are cockeyed, and their jerseys are way too big. They cannot be more than five or six years old in the photo. The two mini-gridiron warriors stand in the backyard, surrounded by a pile of leaves that are freshly raked, and the pigskin is perched at their feet. In those days, they would run endless pass routes, and either John's dad Tom or I would throw the football until it got too dark to see. Neither boy wanted to come inside, and it often took threats by their mothers to get the two burgeoning pros into the house.

Not too long after that picture was taken, we moved to Michigan, a half-day's drive from Chicago. While Andy played Little League baseball and Pop Warner football, something changed the moment he got a basketball in his hands. Around the age of eight, we had moved into a mobile home perched in a trailer park. (After living in a motel for a year, this was like moving into a mansion.) And just a few yards from the place was a basketball hoop. It didn't take long for my dad to get a new ball for his grandson for Christmas, and as soon as the snow receded for the year, Andy was out on the asphalt court, throwing the orange orb up with all his might—sometimes reaching the rim, other times not. Warm weather brought one-on-one father-and-son games, and while I had the advantage over him for a few years, it was becoming evident to this reporter that at some point I would be in big trouble. Andy, on the other hand, learned how to get around, under, and over a bigger opponent and started to make moves that no one could teach.

Watching a junior-high basketball game (or any sport for that matter) is a combination of parental obligation, patience, and muted pride as the not-fully-formed young humans scamper up and down the court, their bodies bursting with testosterone and sweat. It's an odd array of growth patterns on display, and while they take the game so very seriously, you know as a parent that the heartbreaking loss will most likely be forgotten by the time you stop at the fast-food drive-in after the game. The parents usually sit huddled together like a herd of yak, urging their foundlings onward, no matter the score or how long the drive. As a card-carrying member of that group, I salute any mom or dad who has endured "butt coma" from sitting too long on bleachers stained with soda and mustard and has ingested various forms of snacks, candies, burnt popcorn, and hot dogs held in buns that taste vaguely of Lysol. Countless dollars are spent on tape, pads, mouth guards, shoes, wristbands, headbands, socks, and replica jerseys. And gallons of gasoline are consumed to run back and forth to practice and games, all the while mumbling under our breath that this kid better become a pro someday to pay back the cash outlay. If you are a sports parent, I feel your pain . . . and your pride.

Of course, the years and seasons roll by, and the next thing you know, eight becomes eighteen, and basketball has become his Holy Grail. My son's body has gotten longer and leaner, just over six feet, and a scratch of peach fuzz sprouts from his chin, something he proudly points out to anyone who will listen. The bloodline has begun to show itself. His hands look exactly like mine, as do his size 13 feet, much to his dismay. His back has begun to broaden, and the muscle tone is reaching its peak after so many jump shots and laps around the gym. His eyes are clear and focused. His laughter is quick. And he has no problem hugging his father and saying, "I love you, Papa John" in front of his friends, a major evolutionary step from how I talked to my dad at that age. He looks right at home behind the wheel of his '97 Aurora, in which I used to tool around. It has more than two hundred thousand miles on the odometer, but the stereo works great, especially when his iPod is hooked into the dash and is pounding out some jam from some guy I never heard of. (To be fair, I heard it through the grapevine that a couple of John Denver songs got into the mix somehow. Score one for the old guy who grew up in the seventies!)

And so this story begins on an evening that seemed as if it would be like any other night of basketball. The crowd streamed into the gymnasium, buying their "50-50" tickets at the door in hopes of cashing in big. (If you win the raffle, you get half the winnings, and the school gets the other half. Keep in mind that tickets are a buck at most, and if you get one hundred humans at a game, that's a lot. So, most nights the winner takes home around fifty bucks. Some nights, you would do better to take the spare change out of your car's ashtray.) It's an amazing crowd to watch—the local parents, grandparents, family members, teachers, and, of course, the opposing team's fans. They're all rabid fans to the core for the kids, as intense and on the referees as any pro sporting event. You couldn't pay me enough to be a "zebra" and call a high-school basketball game—the fans are way too vocal and way too close.

I recognized the music when it started because, for some time, my son has taken on the role as the guy who selects the tunes and burns the CDs for the introduction. By the time the throngs in attendance heard it, it had been blasted on the home computer speaker seven gazillion times. The opposing team came out first, followed by our local heroes with their purple, gold, and white uniforms flashing under the fluorescent lights. Splitting into two lines in order to encircle the entire court, they met in the middle to high-five as they passed each other, and then they began the warm-up prior to tipoff. The energy began to rise as the music pounded away, and the clock began its countdown.

During warm-ups, I always think about how most of these young men will not play hoops in college and certainly not in the NBA. This is their moment to shine, the time to be on top of the heap, if only for the length of a high-school season. Soon enough, the seniors now at the head of the class will once again become freshmen at the bottom in college. The magical world of high school gives way to the real world of change, but for now, it's their time in the spotlight.

For as long as he has stood for the national anthem alongside his teammates, Andy's head has hung down with his hand over his heart while the others look up or in the stands. I always figured he was getting mentally ready for the game, but when I asked him once why he looked down, he simply replied, "I am thinking about all the men who have been in my life and did great things but are not here anymore, like Hawk (wrestler Michael Hegstrand), Walter (Walter Payton), and Papa (my dad). I ask them for help to be great, too." It was not the answer I had expected . . . how old is he, really?

In the past couple of years, Andy has been up front for the tip-off due to the fact that a mad scientist must have grabbed him and inserted some sort of spring-loaded device in his legs. The kid has a ridiculous standing vertical jump, and I have seen him hit the top of his head on the backboard ten feet up when going for a rebound. I wish I could claim some sort of responsibility for his prowess, but I am for the most part earthbound. The only time I really jump is when a late-night airing of *Night of the Living Dead* creeps up on me unexpectedly. I can access memories from the past when I was over-the-top athletic in my own way and in my own time, but while I was a standout football player, the kind of movement it takes to bury a running back is totally different from having five opposing players try to rob you from glory by shooting a ball into a hoop just slightly bigger than the ball itself.

So, the game started, and our side got the ball. For the first two quarters, it was pretty much standard back and forth, give and take. Each side had its share of shots that seemed to secure the lead, only to be tied up on the other team's equally impressive run. Half-time brought out the 50-50 winner, more music, and fans gathering in small groups to catch up on local gossip, dissect the shortcomings of the first half, and talk strategy for winning in the second. The fifteen minutes passed quickly, and the combatants were back on the court, ready for round two.

By this time, bleacher butt was becoming apparent in the stands. No amount of shifting or sliding, even the short period of standing, brought much comfort. Of course, once the game heated up, all thoughts of posterior pain vanished and full focus was on the court. With another quarter gone, eight minutes of play remained, and both sides kicked into high gear. Full court presses, short quick passing, and the kids became a blur of colors under the lights. I am always amazed at how fast a game moves as it nears its end.

Suddenly, our guys stole the ball on the near side of the court, and it was off to the races! A kid with blond hair matted by sweat and sticking out at wild angles charged down the far side of the court, just steps ahead of the defense and closing rapidly on the opposing team's free-throw line. As he hit the line, the stolen ball had by now attracted a flock of bad guys. He saw that Andy was open and lofted the ball in a perfect arc to the middle of the "paint"—that area between the free-throw line and out of bounds, usually painted the home colors, where most of the pushing and shoving goes on. It's No Man's Land and not for the faint of heart . . . or anyone over eighteen.

Time seemed to stand still. My kid used his built-in springs to leap in perfect timing . . . grabbed the ball out of the air . . . continued to fly *through the paint* while moving the ball over and under two defenders . . . and then hung motionless just a foot from the basket. He then proceeded to lay the ball in the hoop without the net ever showing evidence that it had passed through.

Fans on both sides of the court were silent after watching this not-fully-grown human defy gravity. It seemed like an hour passed, but in actuality it was only a moment or, at the most, two. But it only took one for me to see what had happened. The crowd burst forth with a riotous roar, and Andy ran back to go on defense, as if spending time hanging in space were all our birthright and it was no big deal.

The game continued, and our guys won in a fairly close contest. That was all well and good, but my mind was fixed on that one moment when I watched Andrew John—the baby who lay on my chest at just a few months old in the sunshine while we both took a nap, the little man who had to get stitches in his mouth and tongue when he fell off his highchair, the kid who grinned from ear to ear when he caught two fish on the same line, the young man who is concerned about why kids in this country go hungry when there is more than enough to go around, and the kid I have watched grow from a spindly-legged infant to a broad-shouldered young man—do something that I absolutely know from the bottom of my being that no male or female in the history of our family has ever done.

There are two things that distinguish humans from all other species of mammals. First, we have the ability to change the course of our lives by acting on our thoughts (for better or for worse), and the environment in which we live does not bind us. That is, our circumstances do not have to determine our reality. Second, in the human world, nothing has meaning in life except for the meaning we give it. The value of something—our lives, for example—is totally up to our interpretation. That being stated, we come to this life and are filled during our formative years by all manner of beliefs from well-meaning (and otherwise) sources of "meaning" (parents, grandparents, and relatives, not to mention—but I will—the media) and then spend the rest of our lives trying to undo the "meanings" that no longer fit our soul's growth pattern. In nature, it often takes millions of years for a creature to evolve some sort of appendage to ensure its survival. But humans, with the right information and action, can evolve in the space of a moment, therefore allowing the option for change for everyone who witnesses and follows the movement. What does all this have to do with a gangly eighteen-year-old who loves to play hoops? Simple.

I never knew my great-grandfather, Joe. I barely remember my grandfather, John. And while I have vivid memories of my dad, my son does not have those references as I do. The moment he broke from the ranks of the mechanics, construction laborers, bankers, and radio talk-show hosts that came before him and soared through the air, a new course of what is possible was set for him and whoever will follow. Without even knowing it, Andy proved that evolution *and* creation are, in fact, working in perfect order.

My dad was there when I was born, and I stood over him as his eyes closed for the last time. I was there when Andy came into the world, and I hope it is part of the plan to have him there when my Earth-suit gets recalled. I have had my share of "near-life moments." (Most people refer to them as near-death experiences, but for me those events brought me more alive than ever.) And there was a time when I was sad about leaving the party called life. But after watching my son fly through the air with the greatest of ease, I have little concern if Andy is also grounded. It was while watching *Coach Carter* that he grabbed a pen and paper to write down this quote he heard in the movie and exclaimed to the Old Guard, "This is what it's all about."

Our deepest fear is not that we are inadequate. Our deepest fear is that we are powerful beyond measure. It is our light, not our darkness, that most frightens us. Your playing small does not serve the world. There is nothing enlightened about shrinking so that other people don't feel insecure around you. We are all meant to shine as children do. It's not just in some of us; it's in everyone. And as we let our own lights shine, we unconsciously give other people permission to do the same. As we are liberated from our own fear, our presence automatically liberates others.

—MARIANNE WILLIAMSON

6

The Corner

It's raining. Matter of fact, it has been raining all night; one of those slow, steady, soaking rains that urge the night crawlers onto the sidewalks and driveways and seem to ensure that the color green stays around as long as possible. I woke up a couple of times in the night and listened to the steady baptism from above on the roof, like so many snare drums being pounded on in a rapid fashion. The first time I awoke and listened, I thought about how incredible this planet is—that it regulates itself regardless of how much junk we put in and on it. The clouds move in a pattern that pick up and drop water as needed, according to the laws of nature, not the laws of man. I thought about the process that the Earth goes through to maintain its systems, the aquifers, the rivers and streams, the lakes, seas, and oceans, and how water, without question, is becoming the most sacred commodity in the world— perhaps in the history of the world. This ongoing gentle shower that most of my neighbors slept through would be cause of communal celebration in drought-stricken areas or places where clean water is nearly extinct. I thought about the fact that this water that was traveling from so far above to take up temporary residence in my lawn is the same water that was here when dinosaurs ruled the Earth. *Amazing.* Then it was off to the land of nod thanks to the H_2O symphony.

Not too much later, the smell of the rain woke me again. The first thing I thought of was another time when that smell was in the air . . . a rain-soaked summer afternoon in 1970 on a street corner near my home . . . and the moment that a hero made a skinny, blond-haired boy's dream come true—more than twenty years later.

The legend says that since, well, at least *forever,* kids have waited at The Corner for the boys of summer to stop on their journey out of the city. For decades, young fans would line up for a glance at their heroes, a handshake, or the most sacred of all things baseball . . . an autograph. The key was to get a good spot, and that meant hustling. By the time Cubs broadcaster Jack Brickhouse finished his *Tenth Inning* post-game show, you had better be on the curb with glove, pen, and paper in hand if you wanted any chance at touching baseball royalty. And by 1970, the Chicago Cubs had become just that (if only in the mind of a twelve-year-old boy).

The previous year, during the ill-fated 1969 season, the boys in blue had made the pennant run, and the city was awash in Cub Fever. My mom (who was a rabid Cubbie fan) would give me ten bucks (serious cabbage back then) for a day at Wrigley Field—the holiest of baseball cathedrals. It was an all-inclusive ten-spot that got me on the bus down to Clark and Addison, then into the left-field bleachers where yellow-helmeted "Bleacher Bums" would cheer on the home team and verbally assault the opposing teams. I am sure that my forays into the vine-covered outfield were the first times I learned a few words that my parents did not approve of when repeated. It was about hot dogs with brown mustard, cold Coca-Cola, and making sure that I didn't miss announcer Pat Pieper's gruff voice when it barked out on the park loud-speakers: *"Attention . . . your attention, please . . . please have your pencils and scorecards ready for the correct lineup of today's game!"* I had to get the order right, you know, even though their names and positions were etched in my young mind. *"Leading off and playing shortstop, Don Kessinger . . . batting second and playing second base, Glenn Beckert . . . batting third and playing left field, Billy Williams . . . batting fourth, third baseman Ron Santo . . . batting fifth and playing first base, Ernie Banks . . . batting sixth and doing the catching, Randy Hundley . . . up seventh and playing right field, Jim Hickman . . . batting eighth and playing center field, Don Young . . . and batting ninth and pitching today's ballgame, Fergie Jenkins!"* This band of legends was coached by another legend, Leo Durocher, and we held on to the dream of the big show that year, until the New York Mets caught us late in the season, went on to the World Series, and finally broke the fever. Maybe that's why even today I can only endure a few days in New York when travel takes me there.

I am sure that it was the time I sat in left field next to a couple of hard-hat Bleacher Bums waving the "stars and bars" Rebel Flag in the summer of '69 and the ensuing home run that catcher Randy Hundley clobbered that made him an instant hero to me. After that game, I had my mom put Hundley's number 9 on every shirt I could find, and immediately I took the position no one else wanted in our pickup baseball games: directly behind home plate. Shortly thereafter, my cousin Rich showed up at the house with brand-new catcher's equipment, from mask to shin guards, and there was no question in my mind that I was the heir apparent to the great Randy Hundley!

It was a seventh-inning rainout against the fledgling Montreal Expos in 1970, and while the fans began to make their way out of the park, I made my way out the door. Just a few minutes later, I was standing on The Corner beneath a humongous oak tree trying to keep dry. All the required tools were on hand: a new pen, my official Randy Hundley catcher's mitt, and a small address book that I had autographs in. I waited.

A good twenty minutes went by before I realized that there would be no competition for autographs that day. As the rain intensified, the fair-weather fans stayed home, and I had the Promised Land all to myself. I kept a keen eye open for any telltale signs that the drivers who stopped at the crosswalk on their way to the highway might be Cub players. We knew that Glenn Beckert sometimes wore a sailor-type hat with the sides down and that Ron Santo looked cool in mirrored shades. Some cars had a sticker that indicated they parked in the players' lot and were not mere mortals. You had to be on the ball if you wanted to score!

A few guys came by and waved in my direction with a look on their face that said, "Is this kid nuts standing around in the rain?" Almost an hour elapsed, and I figured it was time to hang it up for the day. I was 0–4, no autographs, handshakes, or high-fives. As I turned to leave, my eyes caught a flash of red heading my way. It was a Corvette . . . and I knew who drove it. As the muscle car came closer, I saw the front license plate: CUB 9. It was Randy Hundley!!!

The Rebel pulled his car over to the curb, and the window came down. "What in the Sam Hill are you doing standing out in this storm for, boy?" he drawled in his thick Virginia accent. With my knees knocking and body shivering from both the damp downpour and the fact that the greatest catcher in the history of Earth was an arm's length away, I said something like, "Waiting for an autograph, sir."

The next few minutes were a blur. "Get in, son. You're going to catch your death of cold." There I sat in the car, staring in amazement as Hundley signed the mitt and address book, while I dripped all over his leather seats.

"Where do you live?" he asked.

"Right up the street."

"Then get going, kid, or you'll miss supper!"

I hopped out on his orders, and Hundley made a hard left turn and was off to the races. I stood there not knowing what to do. No one was going to believe that I had sat in The Rebel's Corvette! I burned rubber on my Keds all the way home, went up to my room, and sat on the bed. I was soaked to the bone, but I pounded a ball into the newly signed mitt and felt like the baseball gods had granted me entry into the field of dreams. What a moment.

Twenty-two years rolled by. The boy of twelve was now a married young man of thirty-four and trying to make his way in the world with two kids and all the responsibility that comes with family. Somewhere along the line, he was asked if he would be interested in writing an article for a Chicago sports magazine about what it would be like to play baseball with the big leaguers as part of what is called a "fantasy camp." And who might be the creator of those camps? One Cecil Randolph Hundley, former Cub catcher and All-Star! With shaking knees and memories of The Corner, I accepted.

I called Randy Hundley's Fantasy Camp and heard that familiar drawl. We made arrangements for me to play in a three-day camp that would culminate with a game in full uniform at the "friendly confines" of Wrigley Field. I did not say anything to Randy about The Corner . . . I wanted to do that in person. A few days later, I checked in at the baseball diamond at the University of Chicago where we would train for the first two days along with about forty other "rookies" who had signed up to live their baseball dreams. There, standing in the bright sunshine with clipboard in hand and a big blue number 9 on his back, was the man who made one-handed catching the major league standard, the man who caught more games than anyone else during the 160-game seasons, and the man who signed my mitt so many summers before.

I summoned my courage and called his name. "Hey, Randy!" Hundley spun on his heels. "C'mon, rookie, let's move it! You're five minutes late. That could cost you fifty bucks and fifty laps!" Then he grinned. "Get in line, man." This was going to be good.

Randy quickly broke us down into two squads. I was on the team coached by the great Gene "Ollie" Oliver, who was a pretty fair catcher in his own right and held the distinction of being traded for the legendary Bob Uecker. We had our marching orders, and now it was off to the locker room to suit up. We must have looked like a group of schoolboys that got let out early when we descended into the locker room to find our uniforms hanging in a locker with our name above it. It was the familiar white jersey and pants with the blue pinstripes, the blue cap with a big red C on it, and the blue stirrup socks that completed the outfit. While I was a late addition to the roster, the number I requested was sewn perfectly on the back of the jersey, as if my mom had done it herself. I was finally wearing the coveted number 9 for real, or as close to real as I could get.

Just as we readied to take the field, I found Randy in the dugout and thanked him for the opportunity. I assured him that the article would be great. Then I asked him the big question. Did he remember having me sit in his car and signing my mitt in the middle of a downpour after the Expo rainout? Randy thought for a moment and said, "Naw, I don't remember that." He turned to the batter's box, but then looked back and said, "That was you? Naw. Now forget that stuff and get ready to run some sprints, rookie!" As I trotted out to right field, I could see him working it over in his mind. I never did get a direct yes or no answer.

We shagged balls and learned the right way to spit, steal, and slide. I drove home from the first day knowing that tomorrow would bring me one day closer to playing in Wrigley, but it also meant that I would most likely need help to get out of bed after using muscles that I had forgotten existed. The second day was much like the first, with drills and more drills, and then we broke down for a real game after lunch. Ollie challenged us to cream our opponents and make him look good, and we gave it our all. As the game came down to the last inning, we were losing by three, and I was more focused on playing downtown the next day, not this warm-up match. I was dreaming about Wrigley when I realized that I still had one more at-bat, and by the time I stepped up to the plate, the bases were loaded and with two outs. I was either going to be a loser or a hero, and to make matters worse I was facing the dreaded Iron Mike.

Iron Mike had deadly speed and accuracy, and he never got tired, even this late in the game. It was a pitching machine! One of the pros stood behind Iron Mike and fed the ball into the arm, setting it for whatever ball he wanted thrown—curve, fastball (could never hit the hanging curve), or change-up. The sky was overcast and threatening rain, and with the count two and two and down by three, I looked to the dugout. Ollie gave me the sign to swing away (What else was I going to do?), and Iron Mike delivered a fastball right down the middle of the plate. Yours truly promptly nailed it right in the sweet spot and deposited the ball over the left-field fence, about twenty rows up and a distance of about 375 feet! As the rain began to fall, the bases cleared, and I slowly made my way around first and past second, pausing to give a high-five to the third-base coach and jog the last few feet into the throng of teammates that had gathered at home. What a rush! The camp photographer clicked away and froze a moment in time . . . Ollie bear-hugging me just after crossing the plate and me with a big ol' grin on my face. You would have thought we had won the World Series! There were no aches or pains to be found that night.

The next day, we entered the Wrigley shrine, and after getting dressed, we took the field to warm up before our game with the pros. While the guys ran sprints in the outfield, I took a few moments to wander over to home plate. I stood behind the bright white rubber base and squatted down. *This is where Randy Hundley caught so many games in the summer heat. It's where names like Johnny Bench and Gabby Hartnett called for the high, hard one inside.* I looked to dead center at the giant green scoreboard and farther below to the ivy-covered walls, and then to the box seats down the third-base line that were just starting to fill up with friends and family who had been invited to the game. I could hardly grasp that the dreams I'd had as a young boy had, in fact, come true.

The game, however, snapped me back to reality. Word, of course, got out that the rookies had a slugger, and there was no way that the pros were going to lose this one. Matter of fact, according to Randy, they had never lost a game. So every time I came to bat, the boos and catcalls got louder. Randy, who was catching, either untied the laces on my cleats or kept throwing dirt on my shoes, and the ump turned a deaf ear to my protests. By the time we got to the sixth inning (we played seven), I was one for two with a single to show for my efforts. Up to that point, the pros had rotated pitchers (no Iron Mike this time around), and as I came up for my final at-bat, we were down by one with two men on and two outs. Here we go again!

Hundley called time, and in from right field trotted Rich Nye, a six foot four, hard-throwing southpaw who had won thirteen games for the Cubs one year and is a respected veterinarian when he is not trying to make guys like me look bad with a bat. He was set to replace Larry Biittner, who had been hurling up to that point. Hundley and Nye conferred on the mound, and Randy trotted back to his position behind the plate and said, "Ready for some big-league pitches, rookie?"

"Bring it on," I said. Not the wisest words I have ever spoken, by the way.

I never saw the first pitch. It was only when it made a "thump" in Hundley's mitt that I even knew the ball had been thrown. This was serious stuff. Then I took an outside pitch low and away for a ball and fouled off the next two. With two outs, the runners would be moving. Could I do it two days in a row? I looked at Ollie in the dugout, who gave me a thumbs-up. Nye reached back and hurled the ball toward home. I had a bead on it. I swung right at the moment the ball was going to cross the middle of the plate, but hit nothing but air. The hanging curve had claimed yet another victim. I could feel the goat horns growing on my head.

"Grab some pine, rookie," barked Hundley, meaning that there was a place on the bench with my backside's name on it. I trudged back to the dugout and caught the gaze of my young son Andy in the stands sitting on my father's lap. But all I could do was smile. It didn't matter that I had struck out because I had done it on the field of dreams.

Of course, we lost the game, but all was made right at the evening event when each of the rookies was presented with a signed ball and a million-dollar contract, and treated to a great meal with the pros. To top off the evening, comedian Royce Elliott had us in stitches for the remainder of the night. As the event came to an end, I sought out Randy and thanked him for creating a space for guys like me to spend time with guys like him. Randy said, "You know, John, you never know what will happen if you hang around the right street corner," and with that we shook hands and called it a night.

I wrote a pretty decent article for the magazine about what it was like to be a rookie for three days—the gags the pros played on us, the friendships that came out of the experience, and the pulled muscles that had to be worked out. I wrote about wearing number 9 and creaming one into the left-field seats. And, finally, I wrote about how important it is to hold on to your dreams, no matter what, because they can come true in their own place and time. I have stayed in touch with Randy over the years. He has been a frequent guest on my show, and he always hates to admit over the airwaves that I hit the only grand slam in fantasy-camp history. Man, did I cream that one.

These days, I split my time between home in Upper Michigan and home in Chicago. My Windy City digs are just a few blocks from the grammar school I attended, and every morning on my way to the Kennedy expressway, I stop at a four-way intersection. One of those corners was my turf as an orange-belted patrol boy, and directly across the street is The Corner where legend has it that kids since the beginning of time have waited for their heroes to show up and sign a baseball.

Countless moments have passed since I stood on that street corner in the rain, and while it's not healthy to spend too much time in yesterday, sometimes certain moments that are triggered by the sights, sounds, and smells of today can be a great reminder of how far we have come in our lives. It's like playing a game of connect-the-dots as you remember moments that have been pivotal points and anchors. I always say, "When in doubt, write it out," and while there has been no doubt in my mind about how much of an impact a few minutes can make, it has been cathartic for me to recall so many of the moments that have added meaning and depth to my life.

Visual proof is always fun, too, and whenever my knees hurt (usually before it rains!) or the weights in the gym seem much heavier than I remember, I pull out the pictures of me wearing a Chicago Cubs uniform, squatting behind the plate just like on a baseball card. Or the one of me crossing home after smacking a "granny" and clearing the bases, and the huge grin on Gene Oliver's face. We love our "Kodak Moments," and I think it's because we are able to stop time. And one of the things we all hope for—eternal life—becomes a reality. No one grows old on the Polaroids, and the passing of time is put on hold and finally in our control, even if it's only an image on a piece of paper. I look pretty good in the snapshots, and it will be something to pine over a few summers from now when I am sitting in the rocker looking for my teeth.

On a sad note, Ollie died a couple years ago, and it is a stark reminder that heroes are just people, too. Even with all our technology and smarts, we cannot stop time from marching on. However, when I close my eyes and listen to the rain, The Corner, Ollie, grand slams, and Wrigley Field are still very much alive. Man, I love baseball.

Baseball is like church . . . many attend . . . few understand.
—LEO DUROCHER (1906–1991)

7

Dragonfly

In mythology, dragons are harbingers of devastation and annihilation. They swoop in on armored wings with fire blazing from their nostrils and steel talons poised to wreak havoc on humanity. Measuring more than one hundred feet from nose to tail, with a wingspan the length of a 747, dragons are part of every culture. And while there is great strength associated with this creature, the overall influence on our psyche has been one of fear.

The lowly housefly, on the other hand, does not have armor on its wings, nor does it breathe fire. And, last I looked, it sports no talons. Checking in at around a quarter of an inch and with the wingspan of the small toenail on your right little piggy, they are not of mythological significance. No great tales are told of battles with the lowly fly—even though it seems that once a summer I have to get down and dirty with some very nasty horseflies that live on in ancient tradition. The most closely associated feeling we have for the fly is simply to kill it, for it's all about spreading germs after feeding on its favorite food—you know, shit.

However, something magical happens when you put the names of these two very distinctly opposite creatures together. And a visit from a couple of these winged wonders gave me an unforgettable moment that once again taught me great things.

I am convinced that my neck has a different bone structure from the average humanoid for it seems there is a ball and socket swivel at the base of my skull where most people just have vertebrae. Simply speaking, I am in a near-constant state of amazement when it comes to the world we live in. The slightest movement, bright colors, planes taking off and landing, snow falling, sunbeams, toads hopping, fish jumping, wind blowing— all beg for my attention, and my head seems to move on autopilot back and forth so as to not miss anything on the adventure. How incredible it is to be alive and be a participant in this great mystery! This little blue ball that hangs in space and totally supports the great abundance of life is nothing short of a miracle to me. Not a day goes by that a blade of grass making its way through a crack in the concrete or some small bird singing for all it is worth from the pine tree outside the window fails to serve as a reminder that I am a strand in the web of life and not the creator of that web. Without question, many life lessons have come to me in the form of great friendships, incredible radio interviews, and awe-inspiring performances, but when it's all said and done, nature has always been my greatest teacher.

I learned a very long time ago that nothing in life has any meaning except for the meaning I assign to it. Once you figure out what the things in *your* world really mean to *you,* then your course is set. It's only when other humans attempt to inject their meanings into your meanings that things get . . . well . . . mean. One person can lose a job and commit suicide, while another person working in the same industry gets the axe and it's cause for celebration. Why? *Nothing has any meaning except the meaning we give it.*

Nature, of course, is not in the business of assigning meaning because it just is what it is. People, however, assign meaning to nature in some vain attempt to humanize that which is not human. As I type these words, Hurricane Gustav is bearing down on the Gulf Coast just three years after Katrina wiped out the Superdome. According to a *USA Today* news story in 2007, the once-popular name Katrina was all but knocked off the list of baby names due to its association with the catastrophe. It now ranks about 375th, just below Brenna (which is also a town in Poland, by the way). My grandfather's middle name was Gustav, and the fact that the first time I ever heard that name used by anyone else was on the Weather Channel is a big deal to me. If we are going to assign people's names to weather patterns that have a destructive bent, why not use names like Adolf or Saddam or Mussolini? When was the last time you ran into a kid named Genghis? My point is that when we assign a meaning, there is a good chance that what we *think* it means and what it *really* means are two different things. Know what I mean?

Perhaps one of the reasons I am so filled by nature is that there is no pushback when I assign meaning to it. When I am lying out naked as a jaybird (ever seen a naked jaybird?) on the wet grass after a long, hot sauna, and a shooting star lights up the night sky, it fills me by the simplicity of its design. I don't have to dig any deeper or look any further to find meaning. It's right there for me. I don't have to explain it, defend my position on it, or make it right. It is what it is, and it meets me at the level on which I am ready to accept it.

That's why I know that when a dragonfly crosses my path, it means that the architect of the universe is sending me a lifeline, a messenger, and a teacher all at the same time. Remember, now, it's *my* meaning, not yours.

On one particular day, life wasn't going so great. I was supposedly on vacation, but since I live where many people take vacations

(Upper Michigan), home is where I like to be. For someone who has a deep connection to the wild, it's just this side of heaven, with dense forests, winding streams, open water, and abundant wildlife. On this day, while it's true that my body was not in the office, the electronic colostomy bag at my side (the personal digital assistant, or PDA, that I have now worn for twenty-four months) is a buzzing reminder that vacation, or the art of vacationing, is often an illusion. I may have a four-day growth of beard, dirt under my toenails from walking barefoot in the garden, and a pair of shorts on that should have been sent to Goodwill years ago, but my brain is often pulled back to business matters.

I admit to being ornery, tired, and not my best self on this particular day. The schedule I keep seems to have me in a constant search for balance, and I often feel like a gyroscope that is wobbling toward its last rotation. When that happens, I know it's time to swap the off ramp for some pine trees, the parking spot for a fishing pole, and my computer for a walk in the river. For me, there is something sacred about walking in a cold, running river on a hot summer's night.

But I had a fairly important phone call to make, and as the time inched closer to the appointment, the tired, worn-out, fatigued part of my brain knew exactly what to say. I had it all planned out, and it would have sounded a little like this: "Hey, listen . . . I understand that @#!%#@%$&*!!^. And that &#@&!%&$#*&@. Furthermore, it's come to my attention that ^@%@!*#$@! So I need to know from you what the &#^%@*#^$@!& is going on and what the deal is!" Nice, huh?

Satisfied with my prepared verbiage, I made the call. After five rings, the voice mail kicked in, and I simply said, "It's John. Give me a call when you get in." I figured I'd save the good stuff for the real thing. After I hung up, a name popped into my head. For this book, we'll call her, hmmm, *Katrina*.

"Katrina" had been in and out of my mind all morning, mostly when I was cutting the grass. There is absolutely no association between that activity and this person, but cutting grass, washing cars, and maybe cleaning double-paned windows have the effect of "wax on, wax off" for me. (If you need further explanation, rent the movie *The Karate Kid.*) While doing these activities, I move into this near-perfect Zenlike state (although it's a riding mower, so I can't zone out too much), and my mind begins to do what it was designed to do—connect with the master computer and get busy downloading orders from headquarters so my life reflects the best, not the worst, within me.

So Katrina's name had been wafting in and out, and since my call had been postponed, I gave her a ring. It didn't take long for her to figure out my state of being. "You sound tired," she chirped. "What's up?" I gave her the laundry list of complaints, hurts, and grumbles, how the world was doing me wrong, and then I told her about the call I was waiting on and the message I wanted to deliver. "You're going to talk to this person with all that baggage hanging around your brain about something as important as this? Good thing they weren't in when you called. If it were me and you ran that rant by my ears, I would think twice about anything you ever said to me again." Ouch, that woke me up just a little.

"So you are telling me to fight fire with water instead of a flamethrower (an analogy I often use on the radio, but too often forget in my own life). Is that what I am hearing?"

"What do you think?" said Katrina.

I was now sitting on my rear deck in the sunshine, and in the corner of my eye I spied something shooting across the yard as if on remote control. In short order, a small, iridescent red dragonfly had attached itself to my left shin. It looked to me like a *Sympetrum flaveolum,* or yellow-winged darter (I checked it out online later—although this species is only found in Europe and

China, that's what it looked like to me!), and I remarked to Katrina, "Hey, a dragonfly just landed on my leg!"

She replied, "You know what *that* means, don't you?"

"Huh?"

"The dragonfly has the power to see around things and from a new perspective due to its ability to see from different angles. It's about change and light and movement and being flexible. Pretty cool, huh?" said Katrina, suddenly the bug expert. "I'd say that was a sign . . ."

I relented and admitted that it was a good thing there had been some space between my intended first call and me seeing things differently. The dragonfly went about its business and Katrina did the same, satisfied that she had somehow completed a divine assignment. About thirty minutes later, I connected with my post-poned conversation and came at it with a totally different energy and perspective, without the need for result or resolve. The fog had lifted, and I felt centered once again. Much like Scrooge, who thought he had learned his lesson from the first Christmas ghost, I did not think I would need another visit for quite some time.

Yeah, right.

Just one day passed before there were more tugs on my tether, and the bile had again risen in my throat, clouding the recent memory of clearing. I have come to the conclusion that there is always going to be "bullshit" (for lack of a better term) in life. You know, minutiae that doesn't ever amount to anything but fills up our lives in such a way as to cause level-one brain aches. Knowing there is going to be BS in life is one thing; creating more of it and trying to pass it off as substance is called MBS, or "man-u-factured bullshit." It is mostly known in governmental circles, corpora-tions, and some religions and is associated with mental hemor-rhoids. I have a fairly high tolerance level for BS because it comes as standard issue in the life thing, but zero tolerance for MBS.

And for the past two years, there had been a steady increase in MBS production in my life. I was in a place that had me questioning my choice of career and life path.

Yes, there was MBS going on (because I determine what something means), and the line between vacation and incarceration was becoming rapidly blurred. I had broken my own rule about not getting caught up like a smelt in a gill net, and there I was leaking cranium fluid. I walked out to my car in the garage to retrieve my headset (if I was gonna be on the phone, I might as well do it right) when a weird, buzzing sound caught me off guard.

I could not place the noise or where it was coming from, so I reached through the open window of my closed car door. Suddenly, the buzz got very loud. Looking to the inside rear deck of my car, I found the source of the vibration—a very large, double-winged, green dragonfly pounding itself against the glass in an attempt to find freedom. Time and time again, the insect rammed the invisible glass wall that confined it. I went to the back seat and did my best not to make matters worse in an attempt to get the bug to move to my finger. After a few minutes, I was able to get it to grab the tip of my thumb with its hooked legs so I could remove it. The little helicopter held on with all its might, and I was able to get it out of the car and into the sunlight.

I have seen dragonflies all my life, but this one seemed different somehow. Being a bit stunned by its efforts, he (or she or it) was in no hurry to leave my digit. It was the first time I had been able to do a close-up field study on this incredible creature while it was alive. The translucent wings seemed too frail to allow this marvel to reach dizzying speeds and grab its prey out of the air. The two large eyes had a zillion mini-panels to allow for multiple angles of vision that gave it a distinct advantage over its next meal, and the threadlike legs were studded with mini-spikes that were a great product of evolution. Its thin body seemed almost rudderlike, and the "tiger of the sky" appeared to be ancient and divine, all in the same glance. It went about the business of "cleaning" or stroking its eyes with its tiny forelegs while perched on my finger, and I took a couple of shots of it with my camera to remember the moment.

I had forgotten all about the MBS by the time I placed the insect on a small towel that had been lying on the deck. As it sat there, other thoughts came to me. Like the dragonfly, how many times had I tried to break out but could not see what was holding me back? Had I allowed anyone to come along and help me stop banging my head on the invisible wall? Did I take enough time to gather myself after my self-imposed pounding? Had I been seeing things from only one point of view again? What other "meanings" did this bug that has ruled the insect airways for 350 million years have for me in the twenty-first century? It was off to the Great Wizard of Google for more information.

Guess what? The dragonfly can almost completely turn its head around, as if were is on a swivel. *I know someone like that.* The lifecycle from underwater larva to full-grown adult is two years, and many changes take place in that time. *Two years . . . the length of time of my current career choice.* When one lifecycle ends, another is already beginning, so it's not just the past two years, but the next two as well. *What lies ahead for me?* The dragonfly's amazing head bends and shifts light to create a new vision of flight, in effect changing its inner reality to make the outer reality more easily navigable. *What did I need to change in myself so that the world I live in can be more of an adventure and not an ass kicking?* Finally, I learned, this little creature does not question its existence; it goes about its business with an inner knowing of its purpose. It was a reminder for me to do the same.

As I write this, it is 1:18 in the morning. Most of the Eastern time zone is asleep, and the dragonfly is still out on the deck. My guess is that, due to the cool evening and the numerous times it whacked itself on the glass, its life span is most likely over.

But due to our prearranged rendezvous and the fact that our paths crossed, my little winged warrior reminded me that my life is just beginning. Again. This time, I pledge to see it differently, to keep my eyes open for invisible barriers, and to let those around me help me get on my wings . . . er, feet again.

The two aspects that make up this incredible creature—the dragon and the fly—are distinctly different in their presentation. It occurred to me as I wrote this chapter that the nobility and power of the mythological dragon, if harnessed properly, can move me forward, past the obstacles that would have me small, weak, and feeding off the crap in life. The more I ponder the short existence of these prehistoric flying machines, the more precious my time on the planet seems.

Deep in the sun-searched growths the dragonfly
Hangs like a blue thread loosened from the sky.
—Dante Gabriel Rossetti

8

From a Distance

At times, I am convinced that the line between here and there, life and death, is but a step away. Over the years, I have had several "near-death" events that left me with a sense of "Why me?" But the answer always comes back, "Why not you?" It's an interesting thing about the human species, the whole "everyone-else-is-going-to-die-but-me" school of thought. We think if our name is not in the obits that somehow, some way, we will be the first two-legged creature to make it out alive. The fallout from such a mind-set is that since we feel immortal, we go about the life business on autopilot, with no sense of urgency for the moment at hand. After being at the scene of death a handful of times, it's apparent that those of us who are making the transition usually regret the little things we did not do—make the phone call to repair a tear in a relationship, take a walk to see the sunset, skip the business lunch to just sit in nature (even if it's just in a small park), and a million other moments that offer themselves to us. We are too busy preparing for eternity to have any real clarity about the sacred corners of life. Life and death are our most intimate traveling companions in this experience, and if we can use the latter to enhance the former, then when the time comes to pass, you can take that last physical breath knowing that you have fully lived. But, alas, we often need reminders. Perhaps being witness to a fatal accident is not just about the loss of life, but also the rapture of being alive, and the incredible, invisible connection we call the human family.

The Skaja side of our heritage is a very large family. There are probably nine hundred names on the family tree—basically its own forest. With a brood that large, they are spread out from sea to shining sea, and every couple of years they gather for what most would call a reunion, although it's really more like a convention. Jackie's parents had five kids, and each of them has kids. Her father has nine in his family, and they all have kids, and their kids have kids, and some of those kids have kids. Then you add all the "outlaws" and the spreadsheet goes right out the window. You need an abacus and a really good bean counter to keep track of this family.

A few years back, it was decided that the convention . . . er . . . reunion would be held at a large park north of Chicago near the Wisconsin border. Little did any of us know that what started out as a wonderful day in the sun would eventually bring the meaning of life and family to a level that none of us who attended would ever forget.

As we headed north to the event, spirits were high. The kids were ready. Jackie and I were looking forward to a much-needed afternoon of softball, barbecue, and a few cold ones. It was a massive undertaking to get the whole clan in one spot, but what a spot it was. Tents were set up for serving hot dogs, burgers, chicken off the grill, and a ton of other eats. The tunes set the mood for a perfect midsummer's day, and the softball diamond was in need of a couple of teams. A basketball court tempted the weekend warriors, and a putt-putt golf course was open nearby. It was a made-to-order day, in more ways than one.

It wasn't long before Frisbees were flying, kids were running, old fellas were throwing one back, and ladies were lunching. A pickup softball game was organized at the field on top of a small hill that overlooked the entire park all the way out to the highway, about the length of a football field away. Sides were chosen, and soon the Chicago version of softball (no mitts and a sixteen-inch very hard ball) was underway. I can clearly remember standing by first base and looking to my left at all the activity going on with the various family members and thinking this is one of those moments that keeps life in perspective.

An instant later, the sound of screeching tires snapped me from my thoughts. I glanced farther to my left toward the highway entrance just in time to see what appeared to be a large SUV flying through the air in a corkscrew-type motion a few feet off the ground. It went sailing out of sight past some trees, and then there was the guttural sound of metal on concrete. All at once, a hundred people were running toward the highway, and shouts of "keep the kids back" emanated from the parents. As I came upon the scene, I noticed the utter devastation. To my right sat the SUV, flipped on its roof, rocking back and forth like a turtle on its back. Hanging out of the driver's-side windows in both the front and back seat were the upper torsos of two people facedown on the concrete. In the middle of the road was a badly damaged car that had smoke pouring from under its hood. Screams were coming from inside the car.

While the throng gathered on the side of the road, six of us ran onto the highway in what seemed to be a perfectly coordinated, well-rehearsed rescue effort. Four went to the car to help the people trapped, one went to the restaurant nearby for a fire extinguisher, and I ran over to the SUV to see what could be done. It took only a moment to see that there was nothing to be done. Both occupants of the car had died from massive head injuries. The call went out for a blanket to cover them, and while I waited I knelt down between these two nameless people who had died so quickly and said a prayer for them. Then my wife and I placed a sheet over their bodies.

The cries of anguish from the car caught my attention, and I ran over to the vehicle. The badly crushed front end had trapped a small boy over the dashboard on the passenger side, and the steering wheel had pinned the driver in the car. Another small boy had been taken from the back seat and moved to the side of the road where he was being attended to while waiting for emergency crews. A quick assessment of the situation was not very positive. Gas was pouring from under the car, smoke was billowing from the hood despite the best efforts of Jackie's brother to extinguish it, and the feeling crept over me that this thing was going to blow up.

While the boy was being extracted from the twisted steel, I ran around the driver's side and jumped in the back seat. A stream of fuel was running on the floorboards, and the young driver was pushed back in the seat with the steering wheel nearly impaling him. I pulled on the seat, hoping to break it backward, but to no avail. The combination of smoke, screams, and impending explosion was creating a visual in my mind of a newspaper headline that read, "Rescuers Killed in Attempt to Save Crash Victims." As the passenger door finally gave way and the boy was removed, I jumped out of the seat and around to the driver's door that looked like a folded accordion. I shoved someone out of the way and grabbed the top of the window frame on the door. What happened next surprised me. Without a thought, I gave out a guttural yell and slowly began to bend the doorframe down as if it were made of putty. Along with it came the top half of the door, and I reached in with my left hand and began to pull the steering wheel up and away from the driver. The metal yielded to my efforts, and two of Jackie's brothers were able to pull the man out of the car and drag him to the side of the road alongside the two boys who were being watched over by a group of people from the reunion.

We all moved back to the driveway, and I sat on the curb and surveyed the scene as emergency crews and paramedics roared up with sirens blaring. The SUV had stopped rocking, and blood was staining the cloth we used to cover the victims. The passengers from the car were lying on the grass moaning and screaming in pain while the car they were riding in looked like something from a demolition derby. A large crowd had surrounded the area, pouring out from the local restaurant and cars that had been part of the traffic flow.

There was a collective sense of disbelief about the whole thing. I am sure it was due to the fact that the human brain has a hard time distinguishing between the images we watch on the news of an accident and really being at the site. Years of watching the latest wreck on the Eyewitness Channel do not prepare one for the visceral experience of being at the scene. Most stood around in silence, which made the sobs of pain from the little boys that much more pronounced. Near the SUV, an incredible stillness seemed to balance out the incredulity of it all.

While the images of that day return whenever I see traffic backed up and sirens wailing, one thing stands out more than everything else; more than the smell of gasoline on the hot pavement or the way the red hair of the woman who died danced in the breeze even though she would never comb it again. What stays with me the most is that the whole event somehow seemed preordained, as if all of us were role players in some larger stage production so that a distant audience could see some "lesson" in its proper perspective. I followed the string back as far as my human brain would allow. *Who picked that date and place for the event? When did the man and woman in the SUV decide to have lunch on that highway? What about the car that they hit . . . what prompted the driver to take that route that day? How did I happen to be on the hill with a full view of the incident? How is it that out of the tons of people there, only six of us ran out into the road? And what made each of us take actions that were so choreographed that it appeared we had rehearsed this event multiple times like a team?*

The only answer I've been able to come up with is that how all of this came together is really none of my business. Most of us spend an inordinate amount of time focused on the "how" instead of the "why," and while this day brought a lot of pain and death (just like every other day), being fully alive demands that we not shut ourselves off from the gritty aspects of life. None of us want to feel pain or loss, and yet those emotions are just as viable as joy and happiness. They're all part of the same menu. Spending time on how it all came together is like being on a roller coaster that never stops, taking you up and down, around the turn and back, with an endless list of possible answers to the question, "How did this happen?"

When I turn to the "why," things get a bit clearer. Why? Because I needed the reminder that I shouldn't take the next moment for granted. Why? Because I had gotten too secure in the illusion that tomorrow was always going to be there. When I knelt beside the people in the SUV, I knew that one day my turn would come, and that one thought alone spurred me to a greater sense of being alive and not falling back into the functional coma in which most of us move through life.

Returning to the reunion was very strange. Most of us wandered around, not knowing exactly what to do or say. A pickup basketball game got started, and the energy exuded on the court helped to burn off emotions that were stretched like piano wire. The hugs were a bit tighter when the event finally broke up, and the car ride home seemed to take forever. I could not dislodge the image of that SUV hurtling through the air and the driver stuck in the wrecked car, rivers of sweat running down his neck while gallons of gas spewed from the fuel line. I wanted to retch my guts out.

I kept an eye on the online newspapers for the next couple days, and finally the names of the victims appeared, along with those of the occupants of the car. I felt compelled to contact the families of the deceased, just to let them know that their loved ones were not alone at the scene and had been cared for. Two weeks went by before I received a return phone call, accompanied by an outpouring of thanks for the efforts all of us had put forth. The daughter of the man who had died wanted to send a card, and when I gave her the address and town, it became very quiet on the line. "We have been driving right through your town for the last thirty years, on our way north each summer," she finally said. She knew the local diner and ice-cream stand, and what the bay looks like at sunset. A few short weeks later, on their usual trek to Upper Michigan, the family stopped at our home. I was not there, but they sat for a few minutes with my wife and once again deeply thanked all of us for what we had done. She relayed that her father was a widower, and he and his lady friend would often go on drives. They must have decided to take a trip for lunch that day, and since he was getting on in years, the lady friend, who was a few years younger, would have been the chauffeur behind the wheel of her dad's truck. He rode in the backseat with all the windows down, taking in the sights and sounds of summer. It would, of course, be their last ride together.

I have been in my share of auto accidents—one nearly took my life—so I am no stranger to what happens when speed, metal, and human bodies mix it up. All it takes is the slightest distraction or mistake in distance to change lives forever. I finally connected with the family of the kids in the car. It was an uncle and his two nephews. One of the boys nearly died on the way to the hospital; the other had major back injuries. The driver was left paralyzed from the waist down. When I spoke to the boys' aunt, her voice was full of anger. She wanted to know all the details. Who was at fault? I could not help her fill in the blanks very well. She was glad I called, but I could tell by her tone that a lifetime of caring for two young kids with serious injuries could just about put her over the edge.

A couple weeks after the reunion, the family was together for another event. I don't remember what it was, but when I saw the other people who were there that morning, I thought once again about how each of us played the role we had somehow studied for—without even knowing it. While much of what happened that morning was not of our doing and beyond our control, what was important for me is that we responded as best we could, given the circumstances with which we had been confronted. We could not save the lives of the two elderly people in the truck and had to be comfortable with the fact that we were not supposed to. We did extract the kids and their uncle from a wrecked car that might have taken their lives, but again it seems to have played itself out perfectly, perhaps according to some unseen plan that none of us is privy to. One thing is for sure . . . every time I am close to death, I am reminded of how grateful I am to be alive.

I drive a lot, most weeks putting seven hundred miles or so on the odometer as I commute from Chicago to Upper Michigan and back. I usually travel the same route and see the same things, but every now and then I will stop to fill up at a different exit, just to make sure that I don't get too comfortable with the routine and the mind fog that can be a part of long drives. The energy expended while I am driving goes from fairly low while traveling the highway through small Wisconsin towns, past field and farm as I keep an eye out for four-legged critters, to quite high as I cross into Illinois and the inevitable NASCAR-like pace that seems to permeate the toll-way system as each of us two-legged critters tries to get where we are going seven minutes ahead of schedule. As I fall in line with the other Jeff Gordon wannabes, I always think about the challenge of putting a human with all his emotions and penchant for being easily distracted behind the wheel of a few tons of metal moving at seventy-five miles per hour.

The radio constantly reminds me of the upcoming traffic snarls and delays, and at some point you come across a mile-long back-up that has nothing to do with your side of the highway but slows you to a crawl nonetheless. It's something called a "gaper's block" and is defined as a lot of people slowing down to watch what is going on across the divider in the lanes going the opposite direction. It's very difficult not to look, and the natural response is to swivel our heads to see what the flashing lights and sirens are all about. Sometimes, I think we are just looking to make sure we don't see ourselves in the pileup. Once we're convinced we are still immortal, we are off to the races once again.

I tend not to look anymore when passing the scene of an accident. My thoughts are more often on the people who are soon going to get a phone call or a knock on the door. I think about how the actions of one person always affect more than themselves and how important it is to be aware of the fact that while most of us have passed our driver's test, it does not guarantee that all of us will return home safely when going out for a gallon of milk or to the movies or for a drive on a sunny summer's day. I wonder if the people who are being tended to by the EMTs or covered up by the state police said good-bye to their families or told the people closest to them how much they are loved. I wonder if we will ever learn that moments can be remembered—but not re-created once they have passed.

Our fear of death is like our fear that summer will be short, but when we have had our swing of pleasure, our fill of fruit, and our swelter of heat, we say we have had our day.
—RALPH WALDO EMERSON (1803–1882)

— 9 —

Higher Ground

When you are trying to find your way in the forest, it's always a good idea to find a high place to climb and get a different view of the path you are looking for. When you are trying to find your way in the world, the same logic applies. There are myriad ways that you can gain perspective, but for me the journey has always been the reward . . . especially if that journey takes you past the tree line so high up that when it snows, it feels like you are part of the storm. At some point, you turn around and catch a glimpse of where you came from—and, if you look really hard, perhaps where you are going.

The picture was buried among a thousand others that should be in a frame or, at the very least, an album. My son Andy found it and said, "Hey, Dad, this guy kind of looks like you." I wasn't sure how to answer except for the most obvious response: "That's because it is me." A look of amazement crossed Andy's face as he tried to compare the slender twenty-something in the grainy photo to the grainy forty-something sitting across from him.

"Are you sure?" he proposed.

"Yeah, I'm sure."

"When the heck was this taken anyway?" he said, as he quickly moved on to the next picture.

A quick flip-over of the Polaroid revealed a simple but somewhat smudged inscription: *Clear Creek, Colorado, 1983.* I put the picture off to the side, and we continued down memory lane . . . my eighth-grade graduation with me in a blue and white plaid jacket, white bell-bottoms, black shoes, and a white bow tie. What do you expect for 1973? We moved on to my first car, assorted Halloween pictures with yours truly as the Wolfman, the kids getting their faces painted by Animal and Hawk, the "Legion of Doom." We sat and laughed at the times gone by, but the whole time I kept glancing at that picture of me in the Rocky Mountains, wedged between two huge boulders with a light snow falling down—and a look of contentment on my face that I have not worn enough in the past twenty-three years.

In 1979, the world watched as sixty-six U.S. diplomats and others were held hostage in Iran in a crisis that would last 444 days in all. I was just two years out of high school at that time, and a knee injury and a severe electric shock had all but ended any thought I'd had of playing major college football. I ended up at a Division III school and played football there, but life was not turning out as I had planned. It was a concept that was very foreign to me at the time, for I was certain I was the center of the universe.

By 1980, college had become a chore, and my life was becoming a bore. I grew tense watching this international drama unfold, so I decided to do something about it and join the Marines. But before I could sign on the dotted line, a late-night phone call pointed me in another direction. The day before I was headed to the recruiter, the phone rang in my little studio apartment. It was a kid we called "The Senator" for reasons I cannot remember anymore. He was a lifeguard I had become friends with at the college pool but had not seen for a few months. I had just figured he'd moved on, which he had . . . to the United States Coast Guard. He was now on the other end of the line calling me from

Kodiak, Alaska. "Hey, Augie, joining the Guard was the best thing I have ever done in my life!" he yelled. With my life in not-much-of-a-direction, I took the call as a sign from the gods, and the next day the United States Coast Guard had a new enlistee. It was June 1980, and I was twenty-two years young.

Three years later, I had a couple of weeks of vacation accrued and was in the middle of what seemed at the time to be the end of the world. I had just about a year to go on my enlistment, and while I really enjoyed the search-and-rescue end of things and being stationed at a helicopter base, taking orders was getting tedious for the free spirit I was becoming. Make no mistake, I was as squared away as they come and had been awarded my share of ribbons and medals, but I was outgrowing the service life. I was outgrowing another life, as well, because a relationship was ending, one that had been serious for a time and intense for even longer. But looking back on it now, it was all in order . . . even my broken heart. Then there was Jake, my ninety-five-pound boxer, who had been my constant companion and closest confidant. I'd had to find a home for him because he could not stay in my new apartment. I found a family to take the big guy, and I remember walking down the gangway with the remaining parts of my heart disintegrating into tears. The year 1983 was tough. I was more than ready for a break from the world in which I had been living.

David and I had known each other since midget football. (I'm not sure if that term is politically correct, but it is football for small humans under the age of, say, twelve.) We went to high school together and had remained friends. While I don't remember the exact setup, my vacation plans were to visit my aunt Ruth in Colorado, and somehow David ended up going, as well. There was no agenda except for a week just outside Denver in the town of Wheat Ridge and whatever adventures the road held for us.

My aunt was really glad to have visitors, and after a long day of travel I headed to the shower, which had a sliding window that just happened to look out over the distant Rocky Mountains that were catching the last rays of sunlight on their peaks. I stood there and let the hot water wash away my thoughts of saluting my superiors, blonds with long hair, boxers with short hair, and a jillion other things on my mind. We hung around the house for a day or two, drank a lot of Coors beer (back then it was a really big deal, since you could only get it west of the Mississippi), and then came up with a brilliant plan. We would take a couple of backpacks and some supplies, have my aunt drop us two city slickers off near some mountain to spend four days there, and then rendezvous at a predetermined time and location. It was the perfect plan!

We threw some canned goods and candy bars in the packs, along with matches and a few bottles of water (from the tap—this was 1983), as well as whatever else we thought might be needed. Auntie started driving west, and about forty miles from Denver I saw the perfect entryway—a sheer rock outcropping with a path to one side. This would be our drop-off and pickup spot. We had no cellphones or other means of communication, but armed with an overabundance of confidence we set off up the mountain. I made Aunt Ruth promise not to tell my parents or anyone else unless we did not arrive four days later, which at the time I thought was a bold statement, but looking back years later was the stupidity of youth. It did not take more than about an hour for David and me to realize that this was a little more serious a task than previously thought. Our ride was gone, and we still had four days ahead of us before we could return to civilization as we knew it. We took stock of ourselves, resolved to push on, and began once again to ascend the dark rock that was becoming more treacherous as daylight faded.

That first night, we almost froze to death, even though it was only early fall to us flatlanders. We each had a blanket, but it was hardly protection against the temperature in the mountains, and the small fire we'd managed to keep going for a few hours brought little relief in the way of warmth. I can remember at the time that while I had gone through basic training and been involved in a few search-and-rescue missions as a crew member, not being prepared could easily keep me from my next birthday. Of course, as it has done for millions of years, daylight finally came, and the stone cathedral we had slept in warmed up nicely.

We spent the second day hiking, resting, and exploring every nook and cranny we could find, and by afternoon we had a feeling of confidence about the impending night that would again bring the cold. This time, we were prepared. David and I were able to keep out of the wind and actually sleep the entire night. Surely our "greenhorn" days were behind us now, by golly!

On the third day, we noticed how close we were to the timberline—that ecological cutoff point above which trees are incapable of growing due to environmental conditions no longer conducive to sustain their growth. Since we were mountain men in training, we decided to push even further up and find a peak that we could call our own. But quicker than you can say "Jeremiah Johnson," we learned that what looked "close" in regard to the tree line was at least a four-hour hike. And, of course, the closer you get to the "top," the more treacherous the footing becomes. We counseled and decided that to come as far as we had and leave within striking distance would be akin to getting close to the top of Everest and turning around. We moved forward.

As we edged upward, my thoughts returned to how many times in my young life I had felt I was within reach of the top and not made it—a constant thought process that had been with me since I got out of Aunt Ruth's car a couple days earlier. A knee injury kept me out of major college football, a severe electrical shock knocked me out of college, and my time in the service was ending along with so many other things. I thought about the girl who had been a part of my life for so long and about my dog Jake, whom I missed terribly. I needed to make it to the top of something without sliding down and coming up short. This time, I could actually see the finish line (even though it was becoming harder to do with the clouds blurring the line between earth and sky), and come hell or high water, I was going to touch the top. I had to.

As all these thoughts scrambled through my head, I kept climbing. Rounding a craggy corner and up over a ledge, I stumbled upon a glistening piece of metal with a bluish tint to it. It was stuck in a crevice and standing upright, like a beacon or some type of landmark. It looked to be about three feet long with a nasty point on it. Upon further inspection by the two of us, we realized that it was a "hiker's axe," which is used for digging in deep between the cracks when climbing to pull oneself along at a faster and more sure-handed pace. For the past few days, our gloved fingers and knees had been taking the brunt of the action, so we saw this as another sign from the gods. I yanked out the axe, took a mighty swing, and stuck the pick or pointed end into a crack and pulled. It was like discovering fire! This thing really worked! The tool added to my confidence factor, and I was able to move quickly up the mountain and make way for David to follow in my path. Whoever had lost that axe had made the rest of our climb to the top a pleasure, and it was one of those "right place, right time" deals that boosted our spirits. In no time at all, we had reached the summit.

It was late afternoon, and the clouds that had been thickening surrounded us like a fluffy cotton blanket. While we were well over a mile high in the sky, the clouds had lowered across the ridge, almost without us knowing, and enveloped the landscape around us. There was a fairly flat, large plateau with an enormous boulder on it that seemed to be the perfect place to stake our conquest, and it was just below the peak that we had sought. David and I stopped, planted the axe in the ground, stuck a little red bandanna on the tool and turned to look back east. We couldn't see a thing!

We made camp in a rudimentary fashion, struck a fire just far enough under the massive boulder to keep it out of the wind, and settled in at the highest point that either of us had experienced in our young lives. We talked into the night with the fire throwing off red and yellow reflections that danced like mountain spirits on the stones that surrounded us. The words were about what was going on at that moment and what we hoped our lives would be in the future, with a smattering of laughter about yesterday. I thought about the many changes in my life, and for the first time ever, I felt the need to write something down on paper.

> For all the campfires where I have sat,
> For all the times I knew where I was at,
> For all the times I wanted to be home,
> For all those times I was never alone . . .

I know there was more, but that's all I can remember. It was the first time that emotion had given way to words to convey how I felt about something. After writing countless poems and lyrics, and as I sit here and write my second book, I recognize how important that climb really was. It opened a door that I did not know even existed, to a place where my thoughts transformed into words.

As night settled in, a magical thing happened: the clouds drifted away during our sleep. It was way into the early morning when David woke me up and said, "Wow, look at that!" Across the rock outcroppings and past the maze of roads below shimmered the lights of Denver forty miles away. And just above to our right, the full moon glowed like a giant night light, illuminating the stone castle that surrounded us. I threw a couple of small branches on the fire, shook off the chill, climbed the fifty yards or so to the very top of the mountain, and looked in all directions. I felt for the first time ever that I had accomplished that which I had set out to do. As I looked straight above me at the lunar surface, so close it seemed I could touch it, a part of me wanted to scream at the top of my lungs, but another part me was awash in the majesty of this place. I thought about what it had taken for us to get there and the incredible vantage point that had presented itself—like a medal you win after running a race. I took a deep breath, stretched my arms up to the heavens, and said a silent "thank you." I had never felt more alive than I did in that moment. David followed soon after and held his own celebration; we slept fitfully the rest of the short night.

Dawn brought a change in the conditions as we began our descent down the mountain. A light snow had begun falling that all but ensured the fire would stay out. We gathered our things and began to snake our way down the face of the mountain, this time with David in the lead and me not far behind, each step toward civilization taking me another step away from the serenity and protection of the mountain. What began as an adventurous climb had transformed into a kinship with the stones, and I could see why people who are of the mountaineering type become so connected to these ancient, sacred places. I didn't want to leave the feelings and the thoughts that had taken me to the top of the world. It was while I was processing all that had transpired in those few short days that David stopped to rest, turned upward, and took the picture of me making my way between a couple of enormous boulders, with the light snow falling and a look of utter connection to my higher self written on my face. The mountains had changed another life.

As we passed the spot where we had come across the axe the previous day, it dawned on me that perhaps this tool was not lost by a careless hiker but rather left there for the next person to use on their climb. We decided that tradition was more important than a souvenir and firmly planted the thing just as we had found it, the only addition being the bright red bandanna tied tightly around the handle. It had served us well and was essential to reaching our goal. I have thought about that axe a few times over the years, hoping that the next twenty-something who needed it not only put it to good use, but also added a memento.

It seems that going down never takes as long as going up, be it climbing a mountain or building a life or creating a relationship. We came out a little distance away from the pickup spot, and by then the snow had become fairly heavy. Matter of fact, the exit point from the mountain deposited us smack dab in front of a sign that read, "Welcome to Golden, Colorado"—home of Coors beer and a great statement to sum up our trip. We walked to a nearby ranch, asked to use the phone, and called my much-relieved aunt, who picked us up a short time later. As we headed back to Denver, I could see the front range of the Rockies and the peak we had conquered. From below, it was small compared to some of the other summits nearby, but it had done its job. It had challenged me and given me a sense of perspective that comes from higher ground. It taught me lessons that have remained with me to this day.

Of the three things that weighed so heavily on my mind back then—what decision to make regarding reenlisting for another four years (I didn't), whether or not my girlfriend would stick around (she didn't), or if my beloved boxer would make it in the family I had placed him with (he didn't)—Jake the dog would have the most permanent place in my life. He was my trusty companion for twelve years. It's very interesting to me that so much of life is like looking through a pair of binoculars. When used properly, they bring things that are far away into focus, but when turned backward and looked through from the large end, the effect is reversed, making things look far away and very small. Perhaps that's just the way the past should be seen.

As my son continued to dig through more pictures, laced with commentary on each one, it dawned on me that memories from a long time ago can be reignited with the smallest image or token. Thinking about them again can set you up to learn a whole new course of lessons that you were not aware enough to grasp at the time. And every moment, even the one that I am presently in— touching my fingers to the keyboard, with the faint sound of music from upstairs and the crackle of the fireplace in the family room, holds the ingredients that are part of what make those moments matter.

Back in '83, I could never have predicted the path my life would take, the challenges I would face, the failures and successes I would experience. But during those four days climbing the mountain, I learned that there is more than one way to reach the top, that it's good to have a buddy along for support, that those who have gone before you in the quest often leave behind tools to make the climb a bit more manageable, and that what often seems so important at the moment is sure to be less important as time goes on. This, too, shall pass.

You don't have to reach the summit for your life to change because the truth is that it's the climb up *and* the hike down that change who you are.

He was born in the summer of his twenty-seventh year,
coming home to a place he'd never been before.
He left yesterday behind him, you might say he was born again;
you might say he found a key for every door.
It's a Colorado Rocky Mountain High.
I've seen it raining fire in the sky.
*You can talk to God and listen to the casual reply.**

   —JOHN DENVER (1943–1997)

*From the album *Rocky Mountain High.* ©1972 by Cherry Lane Music. Used by permission.

10

The Jesus Man

Often, there are times in our lives when no explanation can be readily accessed from the human mind's file drawer marked "logical." Some events are just meant to be accepted for what they are, no matter how much the ravenous brain wants to validate or understand or interpret. Some moments are just a blessing, period, and what follows can be filed in the drawer marked "miracles." It is with this in mind that I offer a moment that has only been shared with a handful of people up to this point. While much of me wanted to keep the following event to myself, I would be remiss to leave it out of a book about life-changing moments because it altered my belief about "what is" forever.

We knew she would eventually need a kidney. My daughter, Amanda, was born with *vesicoureteral reflux,* which is a medical term meaning that some of the urine she excretes would be pushed back up into her kidneys and eventually cause scarring of the organs due to infections. There are five grades of reflux, and as Amanda grew older, hers got worse. The decision was made to correct the reflux surgically, but we never got that chance. Just days before the operation, we were informed that her right kidney was toxic and had to be removed. She was only five, and we were devastated.

She did well after the operation and grew stronger, so we relaxed for a time. But monthly checkups reminded us that, somewhere down the road, this little girl was going to need a transplant to live any semblance of a normal life. We went about the business of our lives, but always in the back of our minds was this looming event that was waiting for us around a corner we could not yet see.

Just after Amanda's seventh birthday, we moved from Chicago to Upper Michigan. It was a time of great upheaval and even greater growth. This book is laced with moments from that time, and it is safe to say that the move and all the events that followed are one giant, continuing moment that keeps unfolding more than ten years later.

The move from Chicago put us on the radar of the University of Wisconsin's Children's Hospital, and we made the long five-hour drive from the Upper Peninsula to Madison and back countless times over a five-year period. While there were times when my girl rallied and her numbers looked good, the truth was that she had only one-quarter of a kidney to work with. The kidneys are amazing organs, but that was not going to be enough to sustain her if she was to grow and be healthy. After every trip to the hospital, my thoughts would run to a moment somewhere off in time when a call would come or the announcement would be made that nothing more could be done. Dialysis would be the next step while we waited for an organ to be found. The image of my twelve-year-old daughter hooked up to a machine for a few days each week, one that only delayed the inevitable, was more than disturbing. I prayed deeply for something or someone to help her, some way for her to be all right, to correct the situation and make her whole again.

In the fall of 2001, not long after the events of 9/11 and Amanda's thirteenth birthday, we sat at a big mahogany desk manned by Dr. Hans Sollinger, Chair of the Division of Organ Transplantation at the UW Hospital. Jackie and I sat next to each other, and across from us were my father- and mother-in-law. Amanda sat next to Dr. Sollinger, who looked and spoke directly to her. He explained what had been going on inside her body, the options to explore, and how kidney transplantation works. His thick German accent spoke to my Nordic roots, and the energy and confidence in his voice relayed that we were in the presence of medical greatness.

Dr. Sollinger received his MD in 1973 and his PhD in 1974 from the University of Munich in Germany. In 1975, he moved to the United States to complete a postdoctoral fellowship in immunobiology and a surgical residency. In 1982, Dr. Sollinger pioneered a technique for pancreas transplants, which found worldwide application. As a result, the survival rate of kidney-pancreas recipients more than doubled. Dr. Sollinger also pioneered the development of one of the world's most frequently used immunosuppressive drugs. In 1995, Sollinger was named Chair of the Division of Organ Transplantation at the University of Wisconsin and the Folkert O. Belzer Professor of Surgery. Good guy to have on your side. As we got ready to leave, I looked out the window of the conference room at the bright fall colors and thought to myself, *Better hang on tight . . . this is going to be a ride.*

The next step was to see who might be a donor match within the family. It quickly came down to my father-in-law and myself, and since I was his junior by more than twenty-five years and in pretty good health, I became the most likely to donate. It was encouraging to think that there might be a solution to Amanda's health challenges and that I was the one who could provide it, but darkness loomed in the back of my mind, throwing a shadow over the possibility of saving her life.

Back in 1973, when my grandfather died around the age of

sixty, not much was known about polycystic kidney disease. It is a condition in which cysts form in and around the kidneys, eventually crowding them out and shutting down functionality. My dad was diagnosed with the same disease just after his forty-fifth birthday, and he eventually needed a transplant that (along with other illnesses) shortened his life dramatically. I learned that it is a hereditary thing that doesn't usually show up until your forties or so. My sister had been tested and had come up negative, but I always resisted the urgings of my parents and wife to go, for some odd reason. I did not want to give any thought or energy to the possibility that I might have the disease, even though both men had died because of it. Here I was at the age of forty-three—when the disease tends to show up—in line to donate a kidney to my daughter in order to save her life, and it was possible that I might be finding out I would also need an organ in the future.

Surgery was set for July 18, 2002, and we began a battery of tests—no doubt the most in-depth exam I had had since boot camp twenty-two years earlier. Two days in Madison gave me a clean bill of health, but there was one thing left—an ultrasound later in the month that would show once and for all if cysts had taken up residence in my kidneys. As we drove home from Madison, I was thankful that all the tests showed I was in perfect health, but there was a make-or-break date with destiny just around the corner. I was going to have to really gather myself for the upcoming exchange.

One place that has always been a source of strength and comfort for me is the traditional Ojibwa lodge that stands on the property of Bruce and Pat Hardwick. As mentioned in my first book, Bruce and Pat are the owners of the Hillcrest Motel, a small, ten-room stop in Upper Michigan. Bruce is an Ojibwa elder, and the motel attracts people from all over the world. They show up for many reasons: their cars have run out of gas or broken down in the driveway, they've gotten turned around and are seeking directions, they are stopping to use the bathroom, or they're in town for an event. Something very special happens on the land on which the motel sits. More times than I can remember, people show up without even knowing why they are there, but one visit to the lodge in the back near the tree line brings them a sense of comfort and peace that they had been longing for most of their lives. When I really need to get centered, I go to the lodge and sit for as long as I can, moving from one sacred direction to the next and feeling the people who have been in this very special place. Oftentimes, Bruce lights a fire in the lodge for someone who is ill or in remembrance of someone who has passed. On this particular occasion, the candles were lit for a naming ceremony.

As I understand it, a naming ceremony is about connecting with one's spiritual self, a recognition of the higher being within. We all have our given birth names, but this ceremony honors that unseen part of us that so often goes unrecognized and, even more often, ignored. Once one is named, tradition says that one is given access to the best part of one's self, and the name reflects that person's connection to all things. When the ceremony is performed, people are usually asked to witness the celebration, and that's exactly what I was asked to do on this sun-swept Saturday morning.

I sat in the northern direction for this event. My friend and walking partner, Duane, sat in the western direction. Another friend, Sandy, sat in the east. Bruce sat where he always does—in a large wooden chair in the south. Those who were to be named sat on either side of him. As the ceremony began, Bruce walked around the sacred circle and spoke about the importance of the day. Then he took the hands of the people who had come for their names and started walking in the eastern direction. In the Ojibwa language, he called out to the sacred helpers of this ceremony.

Slowly, he made his way to the north, then to the west, and around to the south, walking counterclockwise, or in the "spiritual" direction. It was when he moved from the west to the south that something happened to me—what that was exactly, I have no rational explanation for.

As Bruce stood in front of the southern lodge pole, I began to feel like I was falling asleep in my chair. It was a warm summer morning. I had my bare feet in the cool sand, and flies were buzzing lazily around the lodge. Suddenly, I was looking down at my body in the chair from a vantage point of someone standing behind the chair. I looked up and saw that Bruce was still speaking, and the ceremony had not stopped. Duane sat in the western chair with his eyes closed, nodding in agreement with the words, and Sandy sat in the east with her feet drawn up under her. Her arms were wrapped around them, and her face was pointed toward the opening in the lodge roof where sunlight was streaming in.

I was incredulous. I was fully aware of everything that was going on, and yet I was looking down at my physical body in the chair in front of me. This couldn't be happening! The sights and sounds were vibrant and real, but somehow part of another existence altogether. Suddenly, I had the feeling of an oncoming presence, as if a wave were about to wash into the lodge. My focus was just over Bruce's left shoulder, which seemed to be the source of the energy coming my way. And then it was as if the canvas cover on the lodge did not exist because the figure of a man simply walked *through the wall* and towards the fire circle. As he did, a thought ran across my mind . . . *It's the Jesus Man.*

This might be a good time to say that while I am a great admirer of Jesus the Christ, I have never considered myself a devout follower in the way a traditional Christian might. The teachings of Jesus have always held more resonance with me—

"The words that I speak unto you I speak not of myself: but the Father that dwelleth in me, he doeth the works" (John 14:10 KJV)—than studying the Bible cover to cover. So it was a complete surprise to me that the "Jesus Man" would appear in a small lodge in Upper Michigan on a Saturday morning. He did not look like the paintings or portraits that I had seen growing up. His hair was more on the reddish side, and his beard looked more like that of a lumberjack than a Savior. He wore a simple dark-brown tunic with a thick rope around the waist and leather-looking sandals. Two things remain etched in my mind—his hands were thick, strong, and formidable, and his eyes blazed a blue color that I had never seen before.

The Jesus Man strode right past Bruce, who was still talking and looking up to the sky, holding the hands of the two people who were being named. In just three or four big steps, the Jesus Man went right through the fire and stood in front of my seemingly sleeping form in the chair. He did not acknowledge that I was removed from the body, but reached out to me as I slumped on the seat.

He clasped both of his hands around the small of my back, and then he said in a very clear, bell-like tone, "John, you don't need this anymore . . ." With that, he slowly pulled his arms back from my body, and as he did so I could see that both of his hands were covered with a black tar-like substance that dripped off his fingers. He stepped back a short distance from me, put his hands together, and smiled broadly.

Next thing I knew, I was awake in the chair. Bruce had moved back to the eastern direction where he had started, and the whole scene inside the lodge gave no hint of what some part of me had just experienced. The Jesus Man was no longer standing in front of me. I looked to both Duane and Sandy, searching for some sign that they had been witness to this visitor, but there was nothing from either to indicate anything out of the ordinary. I sat very still until Bruce had finished the ceremony and congratulated the people on their new names, and then I bolted from the lodge to get some fresh air. My mind could not wrap itself around what I knew in my soul had taken place. Somehow, be it conscious or unconscious, an appointment had been kept between me and this "spirit," for lack of a better term. If seeing is believing, then what I saw with my own eyes was so far beyond my belief system that the only thing it could do was expand to stay intact and not crumble under the weight of denial.

The questions bouncing around in my head were inevitable. Who was this person? How did he get there? How did he know my name? Where did he come from, and where was he going? What was the black tar he pulled from my body? Why did no one else see him? While my mind raced off in search of answers, my soul began to fill with a deep sense of gratitude. Gradually, the questions were replaced with a profound feeling of peace, for it began to dawn on me that even if I knew the answers to all those questions, what mattered most were the event itself, the intersection of time and space, and the sacredness of it all. However, a few answers were not far away.

About two weeks later, it was time for the ultrasound appointment. Jackie and I made our way to the hospital and soon found ourselves in a dark room with a technician we knew (just a coincidence, I'm sure) from our annual camping trips. It was a strange feeling to have the cold gel on my stomach and side, and then have the wand moved over and over in circles, searching for the kidneys and looking at all angles. I kept cracking jokes about pregnancy, but in the back of my mind I kept waiting to hear some sort of report either way. After what seemed like an eternity, our friend spoke. "I am not really supposed to tell you anything— that's up to the doctors—but it looks like there was something on your kidneys at one point, because I can see some scarring on the surface, but there is nothing there now. They look good to me, but you'll have to wait for the official word." Uh-huh . . . I did not need to get the "official word" because I knew that just a few days earlier, I was at the right place, at the right time, and for reasons that still elude me to this day, that which I no longer needed to have in my body was removed so that my daughter could live. Of course, the follow-up to all this is that now, more than five years post-transplant, Amanda thrives, playing college volleyball and showing her scar to whoever asks to see it.

I have tried many times to find some rational explanation for what took place more than five years ago, but I cannot. Of course, the few people I have shared it with have drawn their own conclusions. It was a sign from God that I needed to become a Christian . . . it was a sign from the Universe that healing does not involve medicine . . . it was a sign that Jesus is still alive . . . and so forth. Each of them ran the moment through their own belief strainer and was certain that what they were telling me was the truth. And, of course, from their vantage point, it was. While I am humbled nearly beyond words when I think of that morning, I have worked to not make more of it than it was. While I prayed for Amanda's healing, I don't think that my words carry any more weight with the Almighty than anyone else's, and I also feel deeply that what I experienced is available to all of us. Maybe trying to figure out how to do it keeps it from happening more often. I did not "find God" in that moment, but perhaps *God found me,* which seems the more organic way for a Divine intersection.

As you can imagine, every time I enter the lodge and sit in the big wooden chair in the northern direction, my mind recreates the moment that I have described in this chapter. Every detail of this

Jesus Man—every sight and sound from that morning—becomes alive and vibrant. It's like I live it all over again. That's the thing about the human mind . . . it truly does not know what reality is. Television advertisers are banking (literally) that your mind does not know the difference between what is or is not real. With that in mind (sorry for the pun), consider that the moments of your life have been recorded in the files of your subconscious and are at your fingertips for an encore when needed. Be forewarned that replaying negative, low-level, and non-life-affirming moments over and over again will most likely cause your life to head in that direction. Conversely, replaying great moments from your life—segments of time when you were fully alive, filled with joy, and showered in success—will tend to create more of the same.

And who knows, maybe one day, just when you need it, the Jesus Man will keep his appointment with you.

People see God every day . . . they just don't recognize him.
—PEARL BAILEY (1918–1990)

11

The Last Hundred Miles

It all started as a dream that began to surface from my subconscious mind just before waking. I was walking on the side of a road as it curved along in front of a stand of pine trees. Even though my face was covered in a beard and I wore a backpack, I knew that I was seeing my image in the dream. The sun was beginning to set on my left, indicating that I was traveling in a northerly direction. This snapshot would only last a moment, but it repeated itself many mornings in the spring and summer of 1996. Little did I know then that it was a preview to a series of moments that would change my life in ways I could never have predicted.

I thought I had it figured out, the whole "life thing." Get good grades, work hard, push all the right buttons, meet all the right people, stay late and get up early so you can stay even later, get the degree, marry the right person, eat your veggies. You know, the things "they" say should give you a successful outcome in life. While all of those things have merit to a greater or lesser degree, they are not, in fact, guarantees that life will work out in your favor. Matter of fact, sometimes keeping your nose to the grindstone only serves to give you a flat face, and there is nothing more depressing than climbing the ladder of success only to reach the point when you find out it's up against the wrong wall. Life has its own set of rules, and often those do not line up with what we have been taught in school or even at home, thus increasing the feeling of being "set up" when you have done everything you were told was "right" and it still turns out "wrong."

The year 1996 was one of change. Two new presidents were elected: William Jefferson Clinton in the United States and Boris Yeltsin in the Soviet Union. It was also the year that Frank McCourt delivered *Angela's Ashes* and TWA Flight 800 crashed. Another event that did not make CNN but was filled with change was a walk that I took from Michigan to Chicago and back north again to the Upper Peninsula; a last-ditch attempt to resurrect my life. I had been following all the rules, only to find out that there was a whole new life waiting for me on a barely traveled country road.

In my first book, *Living an Uncommon Life,* I laid out in some detail how my family and I ended up living for a year in a small motel in Upper Michigan. As one who likes to chew my spuds only once, I will not rehash the elements that led up to this event, which kept us sequestered for twelve months and going through some incredible changes. Suffice to say that the year was life-altering on so many levels, and much of it not already in print needs to remain private.

What has not been recounted to any great degree is "the walk." Often, it takes a great deal of time to see things from a new perspective, things that can be easily missed if one looks too closely or too soon. Naturally, I can only speak from my own experience, even though many people were involved. I did not walk alone. Two other men walked with me to Chicago (and my father-in-law joined in at times), and I want to be sure that I respect the experience they had. My wife has her own thoughts on the journey. People who fed us, housed us, wrote about us, or even criticized us, all played a role. Finally, after twelve years, it's simply time to address the moments that contributed to my becoming who I am before they slip away into my mind, tucked behind my son's basketball stats or my daughter's college tuition and the half-billion other pieces of brain flotsam that take up residence in my cortex on a daily basis. Walking from Upper Michigan to Chicago and back in the late summer and fall of 1996 was more than a pilgrimage; it was nothing short of a "born-again" journey that had nothing to do with religion and everything to do with spirit.

The "vision" for the walk began sometime in the spring, and at first it was nothing more than that recurring dream. I had no real thought of exploring its meaning, mostly because I was too busy to notice. Business beckoned, and I was confident that a certain deal-in-the-making was the one that would finally validate all the "get-a-real-job" talk that often wafted my way from well-meaning family and friends. My buddies and I were close to getting this thing going, and my mind was locked onto how to make it happen. A long-planned family vacation took more than twenty of us to Cancún for a week, which was a fantastic adventure, but even there the dream would crop up every couple of days, leaving me just slightly irritated. When we returned from the trip, everything seemed to be in order, but as I have learned over the years, not everything looks as it truly is.

As the business deal unfolded, things cropped up that did not seem right and had been ignored since the beginning. Looking back now, it's crystal clear to me that had I gone in the direction of that business, my life would be vastly different now, although I'm not sure if "better" would be the case. While all of the biz things were floating around, I was asked to give a commencement speech at a small high school in Michigan's Upper Peninsula, to which I readily agreed. However, not only did I have no idea where the school was (geographically speaking), there was no way I could have known how important saying "yes" would be in the scheme of things. These twelve years later, I consider both Chicago and the UP home, for both locales feed my soul in different ways. Chicago gives me the buzz, keeps me on my toes, and ensures that I don't forget my roots. Upper Michigan calms me, gives me pause to listen to nature and within, feeds my spirit, and ensures that I never lose touch with the land. I am convinced that if more people would get out of the rush of things and simply find their own "Walden," they would be powerfully reconnected to their higher self and not feel lost in a world of six billion other humans.

The speech to the grads went fine, with a theme of "good leaders are scarce, so it might be best to follow your . . . self." I was invited to many homes for coffee and pie, to drop a hook in Little Bay DeNoc, or just sit on the front porch and jaw a bit. I felt enveloped by the community, and the good energy calmed the indecision I had about the pending business. The long and short of it is that I pulled out of the deal, much to the dismay of my partners and buddies. That one decision sent me in the direction of closed doors and unpaid bills, scrutiny from family and friends, not to mention my own inner critic lambasting me for being "spiritual" and "listening within," which was not my normal mode of operation.

But there it was, that snapshot in the morning that was begging for my attention, for me to question a higher source than my overworked brain. One morning after the "vision" appeared again, I called my new friend Bruce, who owned a motel in the Upper Peninsula. His son had been in the graduating class to which I spoke. I knew he was an Ojibwa elder, and I began to talk with him on a weekly and then almost daily basis about the changes in my life. As summer passed and no work was to be found, all the favors I could call in came to nothing, and the hole began to get deeper. Finally, Bruce offered a suggestion. "Why don't you move up here?" At the time, it seemed like the most absurd comment he could make in the middle of my chaos. Move there to do what? Live in a motel with my family? While my mind was making a frappé out of his words, a small voice inside me softly said, "Go there." I reluctantly accepted Bruce's offer, and that night I told my family that I had failed them and we had to move from our townhouse in Chicago to Upper Michigan. The next day, my wife and I sat on the stoop out front, and a large cloud appeared in the shape of an eagle. We took it as a direct sign from the Creator that things would work out somehow. It was the beginning of trust on a whole new level.

Just a couple of weeks after a group of "Yoopers" came to Chicago and extricated us, the kids were in school, all our "stuff" was in storage, and rooms 9 and 10 at the Hillcrest Motel were now our home—and would be for just over a year. Jackie found work as a floral designer, and I drank a lot of coffee with Bruce, wondering what in the world I was going to do next. The answer was not long in coming.

I had crawled back into bed, dragging my ass, as the days were turning colder. After making sure the kids were on the bus and Jackie got off to work, I lay there feeling like a short turd dropped out of a tall cow's butt. I had no job, no prospects, no sense of hope or anything that smacked of opportunity. Our cars were about to be repossessed, our bills were overdue, and the strain on my family was overwhelming. The kids were fine because they were still flexible at ages seven and five, but my marriage was in jeopardy, and my in-laws thought I was a real "whack job." My mom and dad hardly talked to me, even though the last time I saw my mother, there was an odd sense that she somehow knew it was the right thing to do. There I was, thirty-seven years old, with a college degree, all the right phone numbers and connections . . . living in a motel. Shit. Sleep was the best option at that point.

All of a sudden, there I was again . . . walking on the curved bit of road, next to the pines with the sun setting on my left. The vision felt sent from someplace far beyond my consciousness, beckoning me one more time. I woke up and snapped out of bed, ran to the washroom, and gazed out the small window that faced the forest behind the motel and the sacred lodge that sits on the property. I was not going to ignore this any longer. I dove into my clothes and ran down to the main part of the motel where Bruce was drinking his coffee. I hurriedly explained to him what I had been seeing in my mind's eye for months. He went into his room, came out with a small pouch, and suggested that we go out back.

We stood at the tree line, and Bruce announced that I had a choice to make; it would change the course of my life should I accept the gift being offered. I could trust the vision and follow without knowing how things would work out, or I could stand and question why the rest of my life seemed hopeless. I surrendered. I broke down and cried. Both of us big men stood in the wind and cried like little children.

A lodge was called that night, and the "vision quest" was announced and set in motion. After Bruce spoke, I stood and talked about what I thought I was being called to do. While I had not known these people for very long, they felt like long-lost relatives. When I finished, a man named Duane stood up, as if pulled by some unseen ropes, and commanded that he would also walk with me. I was dumbfounded; someone else was a part of this, too? A few days later, a third Musketeer would join us: a young man named Joe, who had also heard the call. When we assembled up north, all manner of support and supplies simply showed up. Each of us was given outdoor gear to walk in, cellphones to stay in touch, and, as it turned out, hotels to rest in all the way south. Even my father-in-law, recently retired, volunteered to follow us in his van as a support vehicle (or perhaps to make sure that I did not totally lose my mind and put my family in further jeopardy). I understood both.

On the day we were set to depart from the lodge, about thirty people showed up to walk with us. One sacred moment I will never forget is when Dr. Bob, a chiropractor and friend of Duane's, knelt before us three travelers and massaged our feet before gently taping them and inserting them into our boots. It was as if he were sent to prepare our soles—and "souls"—for the pounding that lay ahead. We walked out of the lodge, down through the side yard, and turned south on US Highway 2. We headed to Escanaba, then on to Green Bay, past Milwaukee, and on to Chicago. It was 330 miles as the crow flies, but would turn out to be more like 450 miles one way, as you cannot walk on the interstate. The first day, we made it the seventeen miles or so to Escanaba, stayed in a local motel, and had to be helped out of bed the next day. Our bodies screamed in protest from the demands being placed on them.

What followed for the next four weeks was a composite of magical moments, sore feet, loneliness, headaches, doubt, fear, joy, and solitude. It was nothing short of a peeling back of layers, a scrubbing away of the rust that had built up over a lifetime, and I began to slowly remember who I was. My steps got lighter as the body began to respond, and my mind grew clearer about what is and what isn't. I learned the difference between lonely and being alone. By the time we reached Chicago, I had been scrubbed clean—or so I thought. We were met by our families and friends at a fire, lit and tended to during the walk, at Northeastern Illinois University, mirroring the one burning at the lodge up north. It was a great ending for Duane, who had to return to work, but Joe and I stayed to walk back north and make the round trip. A few days later, Joe announced that he felt that I should make the trip north solo, so he hopped on a Greyhound bus and was off to the races.

My soul knew that things were about to get serious. With my walking mates gone and no reporters or even motels offered, it occurred to me that this was the "real" walk. Everything up to this point had simply prepared me for what was to be discovered or discarded on the final leg of the journey. I trudged north with my backpack strapped on securely, my beard leading the way. After a week or so, the pack had gotten really heavy. On the way down, it had been stored in the van, but now I carried it. Near a small, cold stream, I sat and emptied the contents out on the ground, taking inventory. A majority of the stuff I was hauling was not of my choosing but rather had been given to me by well-meaning friends for "just in case." It was on that spot that an "a-ha moment" showed up. Most of my life, I had been carrying "stuff" I hadn't put inside me, but had allowed in because of where it came from— my parents, friends, media, whatever. I believed I couldn't dump these beliefs and thoughts for fear I might offend someone, so I allowed everyone else to fill my pack, day after day, month after month, year after year. No wonder it was so friggin' heavy! I sorted through the pile, kept the essentials I chose, and left the rest for someone else who might need them. I walked away from that stream feeling lighter than ever before, in more ways than one.

I am sure that my newfound transparency made me more aware than ever, coupled with the fact that I had not watched a television or listened to a radio for weeks. All I knew of the world was what was going on in *my* world. It was with this mind-set that I walked through the town of Oconomowoc, Wisconsin, one late afternoon on my way to Beaver Dam, where I would stay with friends Dave and Mollie for the night. As I hit the edge of town and made my way past a small lake, I suddenly froze in my tracks. The sun was setting to my left, the road I was traveling curved just in front of a stand of pines, and I had a backpack. I knew this place; it had been shown to me over and over again, burned into my mind like a laser beam. I was standing in the exact spot "the vision" had revealed so many months before. I could not move, and every last vestige of what constituted reality and "normal" beliefs fell away. My circuits blew out, and my soul stepped in. I had arrived right on time for my appointment, whatever it might be. I stood still, not wanting to move, not wanting to disrupt the feeling of completion that filled me. I wanted to stay there for as long as possible. For a moment, I thought the walk was over, but in truth it was just beginning.

The wind came off the lake and pushed me to take a step. As I did, a clear voice in a bell-like tone rang in my head and commanded, "John, go on the radio." I stopped again. *What? Go on the radio? What did that mean? Should I find the local station and talk about the walk?* A second or two later, it was clear to me. I was to "go on the radio" and talk about the walk that all of us are on—life. It seemed absurd at the time, considering I was living in a motel and had no radio training whatsoever. My life was not exactly that of a well-heeled talk-radio host. But the feeling was strong, and as I walked along, it grew even more intense. *What would I talk about? Who would listen? How could I do this?* What came to me is that *why* is far more important than *how* in life. Most of my life had been spent wondering *how* this or that was going to get done or *how* I was going to do whatever, but I did not live much in the *why* of my life. *Why had I been born? Why did I get out of bed each day? Why not me? Why not "go on the radio"!* If you can figure out the *why* for your life, the *how* will take care of itself.

I strolled along to the pick-up point with a renewed sense of energy and purpose. I felt as if the Almighty had made direct contact with one of His children and had put in a major course correction. I connected with Mollie, and upon entering her battered old ride, I heard a voice on the car radio. It was a guy named Barry Farber, talking about the economy or something. I suddenly announced out loud, "Mollie, I am going to do what that guy does. Talk on the radio. I will have a show that empowers, informs, and entertains people. It's going to be about the life jour-ney and what signs to look for on the adventure. I am going to have conversations with some of the greatest thinkers, movers, and shakers on planet Earth, and by listening, people will have the opportunity to see themselves as a part of the solution, not the problem. I won't tell them what to think. I'll just remind them that they have the ability to think for themselves, and in doing so will awaken the dormant powers within. It's going to be great!" I was really jacked up!

Mollie sat there with her hands on the wheel and her mouth hanging open. "Uh . . . sure, John, whatever you say. Maybe you just need a really hot shower and a shot of Wild Turkey to relax. David got a goose today, and we'll have that for supper. Then after-wards . . ." She was talking, but I did not hear anything because inside me the lights were fully on. Finally, someone was home.

On August 27, 1997, I went on the air at WDBC Radio in Escanaba, Michigan. I often joke that for the first few weeks there were about six listeners, and five were friends of mine. I had five shows to make something happen, once a week for five weeks. My *why* was so strong that the *how* always made an appearance, and I eventually went on to a twice-a-week show, and then over to ABC back-to-back with Rush Limbaugh three hours a day, five days a week. I garnered numerous broadcasting awards with a mission statement of empowerment. I believe that if you raise the bar in terms of conversation and content, people will pull them-selves up, if given the chance. Thousands of shows rolled by, and eventually I moved into the role of producer with Oprah Radio on XM Radio to mentor the radio lives of Dr. Mehmet Oz, Jean Chatzky, Bob Greene, and Nate Berkus. It *was* difficult not to be on the air every day—I ache to "deliver the mail," as it were—but I also recognize that I was part of the *how* for my friends. And just to prove that I am not in control of the *when* either, as this book goes to print, I am back on the air, once again proving that evolution and spiritual design can, in fact, work together, if we are willing to allow them to take their course.

I finished the walk a day before Thanksgiving in 1996, and as I look back these twelve years later, I realize that the most important lessons came in the last one hundred miles or so. It was not until I had been stripped down to my essence, laid bare of my former beliefs and thoughts, that I could accept what the universe was offering. There were many moments on the walk that were so profound that I have yet to find words to describe them. Other times, it was just plain boring to walk. Either way, it's a great reflection on life.

There will always be periods when it seems as if you are getting nowhere, and life's a bore. Yet you find that by putting one foot in front of the other, not letting someone else fill your pack, and having the courage to follow the vision that is given you, you can live your dreams. As a matter of fact, that is what you are being called to do. On the trip, you will find out that the "light" the world needs shines from you, but can only be revealed if you peel back the layers and get down to the truth. While it's easy to be lonely in a world filled with despair and pain, you are, in fact, not alone and never have been. *How* are you going to do it? Never mind that. *Why* you take the walk is far more important. Your path is calling . . . can you hear it?

*I only went out for a walk and finally concluded to stay out
till sundown, for going out, I found, was really going in.*
—JOHN MUIR (1838–1914)

12

Like a Rock

Stood there boldly, sweating in the sun, felt like a million, felt like number one . . . like a rock.

It has been thirty-plus years since I was eighteen, invincible in mind, body, and spirit, but every time I hear Bob Seger's gravelly voice crank out the words to "Like a Rock," the seasons are folded back like an apple being peeled. My aches and pains go away, the sun feels as new on my skin as it did back then, and a glint that had been washed away over a lifetime of seeing things I would rather forget returns to my eyes. Looking back has its benefits, and perhaps that's why we even have memory at all—to remind ourselves of the times we have had and the people who have touched our lives in ways that can only have been revealed from a perspective it may take years to see.

Stress seems to find us in one of two ways: either from the outside in or the inside out. In other words, it comes from events that are out of our control or from events that we have control over but go ahead and worry about anyway. It's all about risk. For me, subjecting myself to a Chicago Cubs home game has a very interesting effect. Going to a night game at Wrigley Field is a great way to let go of the day's work worries (in my control) and shift to the Cubs' win-loss record, the starting pitcher's ERA, and how many games above .500 the boys in blue are. (All of those things are, of course, out of my control, even though I think that they would do better by hiring me to manage the team.)

On one particular fall evening, the northsiders were playing the Milwaukee Brewers in a fairly tight pennant race. (The results of the game that had seemed so important that night became pretty much inconsequential, since both the Brewers and Cubs ended up watching the Phillies and Rays play the 2008 World Series—on television, not from a dugout.) I was attending with Johnny Keith, KK, Matt, TC, and Mark, a few of my radio cohorts, which made it all the more fun. I had the task of keeping an eye on our seats and the Carlos Zambrano bobble-head dolls we had scored by being one of the first ten thousand fans to the game. Matt, who had worked at Wrigley years earlier, was always making sure that we never ate the "steamed hot dogs" before the third inning, as he let on that they were leftovers from the prior game. (He would know.) Matt went in search of grilled dogs, leaving me standing alone surveying the scene. Losing seasons not withstanding, there is a certain magic about being inside the "friendly confines" on a warm evening, waiting for the first pitch.

As the throngs made their way in and began to swarm the park, I was enjoying the looks on people's faces as they, too, were letting go of their day. For a few hours, they would be transformed into young people again by rooting for the boys of summer. As I stood transfixed, I happened to catch sight of a tall man walking about four rows above me on the walkway that half-moons the park. My memory banks shifted. I knew the face, and the name quickly followed—Cliff Pierce, the baseball coach at Carl Schurz High School, my alma mater. I yelled, "Hey, Coach!" and he quickly turned his head, caught my gaze, and waved, "Hey, Augie!" Somehow, as a sea of humans was pulling him along, we managed to hold enough of a conversation for him to tell me, "Give Coach a call. . . . He is doing something in October for Coach . . ." And with that, the masses pulled Cliff along to some farther baseball shore and his assigned seats.

To be clear, the redundancy of the word "Coach" is not a typo. The reference to "Coach" and who gets designated as "Coach" is a language all its own. I knew from Cliff's tone that the first mention was connected to Frank Preo, my football head coach, and the second utterance was about Ray Smith, the assistant head coach. Don't tell me how I knew this, but trust me, it's true. The name "Coach" is something you earn, and when you play for a coach and then become one (as I did for three seasons with both Coach Preo and Coach Smith), you start to decipher the "coach code."

The Cubs lost that game and would go on to drop three straight to the Dodgers, further festering the one-hundred-year boil from which Cubs fans suffer. Cliff's instruction to call was all but forgotten as I slogged to my apartment, confident that, even though we lost another one, this was the year we were going to the Promised Land. I guess we'll wait to see what the 101st summer since we won a World Series brings.

One month passed before a little alarm bell went off in my head like some internal reminder that it was now time to call Coach. I found his number and checked in, only to be greeted by his wife, Pat. We had a rousing conversation. She brought me up to speed on what was happening with the luncheon and where it was being held. My timing was good because I had two days to clear my calendar to attend. Later that evening, my cellphone registered a call. When I checked voice mail, a familiar tone barked in my ear, "Hey, Augie, it's Coach. We are meeting for lunch in Arlington Heights at noon on Thursday. Stu is in town, and Ray is going to be there. Hope you can make it." Longfellow must have been thinking of Frank Preo when he said, "The human voice is the organ of the soul," because from the first time I heard his voice, it touched me deeply and gave rise to a knowing that I had greatness in me and something big to do with my life. Hearing it again instantly took me to another time and place.

The year was 1974—in some ways a far different time in America, and in other ways not so different. An unpopular president was on his way out, an unpopular war was raging, the oil crisis had taken hold, and the Cubs didn't make it to the World Series that year either. It was my sophomore year in high school, and while I had played organized sports as a kid and absolutely loved football, I sat out my freshman year because the guy they assigned to coach the frosh-soph team had never even played the game! No offense to the poor guy, but the young purist in me skipped the gridiron and attended the varsity battles from the stands instead, where I witnessed the local heroes knock heads. There pacing the sidelines was Frank Preo, legendary Bulldog head coach. And right next to him was the barrel-chested and intense Ray Smith. These guys were football! Both Preo and Smith had deep football backgrounds, and their teams were formidable, to say the least. The "big guys" were lined up behind them every Saturday morning, wearing the purple and gold helmets, jerseys, and pants. The stands were always packed with fans. This was the big time, for sure, and the place I wanted to be.

When tryouts came around in the summer of 1974, I couldn't wait. As a sophomore, I could give varsity a shot. I had grown a bit over the summer, but was still long and lanky, probably five foot ten and 175 pounds or so, but inside I felt much bigger. Long before VCRs allowed viewing choice, I would scan the *TV Guide* for any of the NFL films and watch my heroes of the time—Dick Butkus, Deacon Jones, Jack Lambert, and others—stuff opposing running backs like Butterball turkeys. I would don my Sears-issued equipment and slam into trees in my yard. My dad said it was fine, but my mom confined me to trees in the backyard so the neighbors wouldn't think I was a whack job. I was lean, I was strong, and football was my god.

When the day of tryouts arrived, my dad drove me to school in his new AMC Hornet wagon (with the Gucci interior, I kid you not) and dropped me off in the midst of a downpour. Although he was not an athlete himself, he could appreciate my eagerness, but when he saw the size of some of my competition, he gently reminded me that I had skipped a year and not to expect too much. Of course, I countered as Butkus himself would. "Dad, how many of these guys do you think run into trees full speed?" He thought for a moment and answered like the practical banker he was: "Trees don't hit back, son."

I ignored his comment and ran into the "small gym" inside the massive hulk of the school, which is a Chicago landmark. Schurz High School is a huge structure that sits on a few acres (not counting the football field) and has a fortress-like look to it. Even back then, it housed more than three thousand kids. I quickly changed into the required dress—white T-shirt and gray sweat pants with black cleats. Equipment would only be issued if you made the team. That day was for sprints, drills, and, unbeknownst to me, a life-altering sentence that pushes me to this day, thirty-four years later.

The rain had let up as we met on the field, but I was still going to be a sloppy mess by the time it was over. Two assistant coaches lined us up in alphabetical order, and there we stood . . . waiting. It was early morning with a slight mist rising from the grass. We could smell the wet earth, and our breath made little clouds in the air. At exactly 8:00 AM, the sound of cleats on pavement resonated off the concrete walls of the fortress and made their way toward sixty young men who were hoping to become one of the few, the proud, and the elite—a varsity football player! As they had done for more than a few seasons, Frank Preo and Ray Smith landed on the field at exactly the same moment. They surveyed the hopefuls in front of them—a handful of veterans smattered among the newbies—as Preo put his hands on his hips, his keen eyes checking out the recruits. Smith blew his ever-present silver whistle and then yelled, "All right, Bulldogs, let's get moving!"

For the next couple of hours, we ran sprints until our lungs ached, did grass drills that had us hurling over each other in formation (otherwise known as "monkey rolls"), and hit the blocking sled in twos. We pushed it along with the two-hundred-pound Coach Smith aboard, back and forth across the wet ground (a little more difficult than hitting a tree). After all that, we ran our forty-yard dash for time and then finished with some hundred-yard-long sprints as a team. What a sight! We were sixty young men in full gallop across the length of a football field a half-dozen times . . . and loving it. We collapsed after the last one, rightfully exhausted, and it began to pour, which sent all of us across the street and into the tunnel that led into the school's back entrance. It was there that nine simple words became burned into my mind.

I stood with all the other hopefuls against the cold walls of the tunnel, soggy and filthy from the black dirt of the field. My muscles ached. Preo and Smith walked back and forth in silence, surveying each of us and sizing us up. I did my best to stand taller and look bigger as they neared my place in line. Smith was flipping his whistle by its lanyard back and forth, wrapping and unwrapping it over his fingers as he marched alongside Preo. Coach's intense dark eyes measured the boys-wanting-to-be-men who stood before him and began to speak in a voice that has a resonance and tone all its own.

"Gentlemen. Congratulations on having the courage to try out for this football team. Being a Schurz Bulldog is not just about football, but a way of life. The purple and gold has a long and cele-brated history of turning out not just great football teams, but great young men. You practice the way you play, and you play the way you practice. It's as simple as that. Today was a good start and there was great effort out there, but we have a long way to go. By the end of practice sessions in four weeks, some of you will think this is too hard and simply not come back. But be clear on one thing, gentlemen . . . THE ONLY WAY YOU LOSE IS IF YOU QUIT!"

The impact of those nine words hit me ten times harder than the biggest tree in our yard and right between the eyes. To top it off, Coach Preo and Coach Smith were standing right in front of me when the utterance came. Smith looked at me and winked as if to say, "Hey, kid, are you listening?" I was listening, Coach, and have been ever since.

I wish I could tell you that I made the varsity team that year. I did not. I was still a bit undersized, and the year off played a factor. So when cuts were made, I was on the list. But it turned out for the best, as I did hit the field on the frosh-soph team (which had a real coach now) and did well. When tryouts came the following year, I made varsity as a junior and would eventually go on to be co-captain of the vaunted Schurz Bulldogs in my senior year with my buddy Tim Anderson. We were the "Double As"— Augie and Andy—and I can still see Tim in my mind's eye pulling up in the alley next to my house in his blue Pinto on game day. Life was good.

All that and more flooded my mind as I made my way to the lunch. Recent news about Ray Smith was not good; he had lost a leg to diabetes. I had stayed in touch with Coach Preo over the years, and to think of either of them as getting older, vulnerable to illness or disease of any kind, was incomprehensible. These guys were titans—immortals—gods, not only in my life, but also in the lives of hundreds of young men over the years. I couldn't wait to see them. I arrived at the sports bar a few minutes late and hurried in, only to come upon a scene that I won't soon forget. As if on display, seventeen guys were seated at three tables that had been jammed together to accommodate them right in the center of the room. I'd had no idea that it would be so large and formidable a group.

I took a quick inventory in my mind and lined up faces with names as best I could. Ray Smith, who looked fantastic, was at the head of one side of the table. Next to him was Stu Menaker, in from the Carolinas and one of the best basketball coaches on the planet. Next was John Nokes, a celebrated Chicago fireman and football coach, and then John Manchester, with whom I played college football and taught at Schurz for three years. (John also runs into buildings that are on fire.) Jerry Pringle was there— he taught at Schurz—along with Rick Szukala and his brother. Rick had been an amazing baseball and basketball player in my class, and I had not seen him for thirty years. A few men I did not know rounded out the end of the table, and then more familiar names and faces appeared. Cliff Pierce was there, of course, being the Wrigley Field messenger in all of this. Also present was Charlie Bliss, who hadn't aged a bit since high school (just ask him). I looked up to him as a player and had the opportunity to be on the receiving end of his incredible passing arm. I also had the chance to play against him in semi-pro football many years later. Charlie is the master of ceremonies wherever he goes and also serves the city as a fireman. John Reed, our track coach, was there, too. He's the strong but silent type who still looks like he could run the mile for time. Back when I was in school, he was one of the most feared men on planet Earth. Rounding out the group was John Jursa, who was our school disciplinarian. And at the head of the table opposite Ray was Frank Preo. "Augie!" he barked. "Get in here!"

Ray stood up as if losing a leg is something everyone should try and hugged me tight. I made my way around the table, slapping backs and shaking hands, grinning from ear to ear. Charlie gave up his chair next to Coach Preo for me, and it only took a few minutes of listening to the conversation when the meaning of the moment hit me. I thought I was coming to see Frank and check in on Ray, but I realized I was really there looking for a very important part of me that had become paved over like a pothole.

In countless ways, I had become lost while wandering the desert of life. I'd been knocked around like a pinball by circumstances, my job, stress, and the strain and pressure that had sapped me of my inner strength more times than I could remember. But at that table, the young man I was, the core of who I am, was beginning to come back to life. And those feelings made me realize how far away from my best self I had become. It took me back to how I thought about my life and saw the world before all the bullshit, the low-level games, the anger, the resentment, disappointments, failures, hard knocks, letdowns, and mountains of crap had been heaped on my shoulders over the years. As Seger wrote: *My hands were steady; My eyes were clear and bright; My walk had purpose; My steps were quick and light; And I held firmly; To what I felt was right; Like a rock.* That sort of strength, a feeling of "knowing," had been missing inside me for a very long time, and finally I could put my finger on what exactly it was.

As the men sat around the table, talking about the well-faded glories and stories of yesterday, as well as the adventures they are on today, I simply sat in the midst of it all and soaked it up. I kept looking at Ray, who had every reason to have become a lesser man due to the loss of a leg, but whose shining eyes told the story of what was really going on inside him. When he excused himself to use the restroom, Coach Preo leaned over to me and said, "Augie, when Ray first found out they had to take the leg, he couldn't wait to get it done. After it was gone, he couldn't wait for the new one to be put on. From the first diagnosis to this moment, he has not complained one time." We watched him walk on that prosthetic leg as if it were the original. I thought about all the things I complain about, and they all seemed pretty lame compared to losing an appendage.

The lunch lasted for about an hour and a half, and it was apparent that there was more than a little reluctance to leave, but someone had to make the move. It was the running man, John Reed, who got up, saluted the table, dropped his bucks on the plate, and made his exit. Permission had been granted to leave the safe haven that the conversation had created and exchange 1976 for 2008. Somehow, the former seemed more important than the latter.

I made my way around the crowd, promising to stay in touch, giving bear hugs, and laughing my ass off. Standing in front of Rick, it was the first chance I'd had since 1977 to catch up. We went back and forth on our present lives, and I remarked to him how much I'd enjoyed watching him on the court way back when. He then delivered a message to me that put the missing piece back in place. "Augie, the thing I remember most about you was that you were the personification of dedication and discipline. You knew what you needed to do and did it, no matter what." Damn . . . I stood back and rocked on my heels for a moment. He continued, "It's about dedication. I bet you are still working out. (He felt my arm for confirmation.) Yeah, it's still there!" I'll bet Rick and I, while classmates, had never said more than twenty words to each other in two years, and now, more than thirty years later, he was saying what I needed to hear. It was what I was looking for and didn't even know it when I decided to go to lunch with the guys.

Ray Smith was next to last on the good-bye rounds, and it was a surreal moment when he hugged me close, told me how much he loved me, and appreciated that I took the time to join him. Of course, I was the one who felt so fortunate to see that the old Bulldog still had the fire inside that gave him the ability to see what he had gained, not what he had lost. I hugged him for one second longer, just to borrow a little more of his strength should I need it later in the day.

Last but not least, the crowd parted enough for me to reach an arm out to Coach Preo, who grabbed my hand and pulled me close. "Augie, so great to see you. So really great to see you." He was saying something else to me, but I had a hard time hearing him because all I heard in my head were the words: THE ONLY WAY YOU LOSE IS IF YOU QUIT.

I hurried to my car and backed out of the spot just in time to see Frank and Ray walking side by side to their car as if they were headed to the football field. I drove out into the gray afternoon, energized beyond belief. The missing piece was back in place, and I knew that I had a game to get ready for. The one that has no timeouts and no instant replays. The one you are experiencing right now.

Dedication, discipline, not giving up, pushing the sled in the rain, running until my lungs ached. Pride, strength, purpose, and passion. Focus, movement, preparation, and execution. Hitting the trees and bouncing off, rushing the quarterback and knocking him on his ass, hustle and teamwork. Believing in myself, my abilities, my contributions, and my leadership. Doing what needs to be done to get where you want to go without fear or concern for what isn't working. Going beyond limits.

It's 5:08 AM as I am writing this page, and I'm getting jacked up just typing words like "dedication." All of us have a moment that sometimes takes years to present itself, a small slice of time that has been rusted over, forgotten, or lost in too many years on the couch in front of the tube or too much time behind the desk with our eyes locked on a computer screen. Even if football is not your game, *life is*—and the same rules apply, whether you strap on a helmet or not.

The quality of a person's life is in direct proportion to their commitment to excellence, regardless of their chosen field of endeavor.
—Vincent T. Lombardi (1913–1970)

— 13 —

The Naked Men's Club

I can still see the kid running through the back streets of North Boston as if his life depended on it. His legs were pumping up and down, his yellow shirt flying in the breeze as he cut around the next corner, urged on by his mother who was leaning out of an apartment window yelling his name. "Anthony! Anthony!" The kid finally made it home and into the hallway while his mom smiled broadly. Anthony made it just in time for a huge helping of Prince Spaghetti, which means it was Wednesday in America as proven by the fact that thirty years after that commercial aired, I still connect the two.

Wednesday is considered "hump day," the bridge between last weekend and the upcoming forty-eight-hour respite from the job. According to the Hebrew Bible, it's the day the sun and moon were created. It was named after the Germanic god Woden, and so it means "Odin's Day," which was pretty heady stuff in the Old World. Ash Wednesday is a very important part of the Catholic religion, and on a completely different note, Wednesday was the night I would bowl with my dad until the wee hours of the morning—all in the name of the father/son thing. However, for the past five years, Wednesday has had a completely different meaning for me. It's the night I get naked with four other men.

Now, before you call your local book retailer in protest or Tipper Gore for a parental advisory sticker on my dust sleeve, let me fill in the blanks a bit for you. One look at the fairly heavy snow that is falling outside my window is enough to recall a night that changed two families forever and sent a ripple effect out into the world that continues to this day, nearly six years later.

If you read my last book, *Living an Uncommon Life,* you might have been one of the many who sent me a note regarding how you were affected by a chapter entitled "Love Lights the Way." It recounts the tragic loss of young life when sixteen-year-old Chelsey Jo Hewitt and her boyfriend, seventeen-year-old Timothy Wotchko, were killed on a snowy February night in 2002 when a logging truck collided with their vehicle. Chelsey died of her injuries at the scene. Tim lived long enough to make sure his wishes of being an organ donor were honored. I had seen Chelsey the night before at a basketball game, and she had just earned her driver's license that very day. Tim was a star on the basketball team, as well as the football field, and was a role model for many younger boys. The basketball coach, Jerry Collins, asked me to speak to the team about Tim's death.

About six months later, I sat in a small church in Upper Michigan in prayer, deeply saddened by Jerry's death at the age of twenty-five, also in an auto accident. Three amazing young people left their families and friends behind, but in doing so they also left formidable lessons for all of us. Chelsey was convinced that if you just treat others the way you want to be treated, life would always work out. Tim knew that you give things 110 percent or you don't waste time because there is no time to waste. Jerry absolutely knew what he had come to this planet to do—teach life lessons to young men with a hoop and a ball. There, plain as day, were the three keys to living an uncommon existence, taught in a way that could not be ignored, but often becomes forgotten in the daily rush of life. No matter what life puts in our path, it's critical to have somewhere to go to begin the healing process. Sometimes we need to seek it out; other times it finds us.

Dennis Wotchko is a gentle giant, with a heart as big as the north woods that he loves so much. He is a throwback to another era as he works the rails to make sure trains do their thing. Thoughtful in his words and careful with his thoughts, Denny is the neighbor everyone should have next door. As the days became months after his son had passed, Denny felt a stirring inside to create a place for his grief to be released. He thought about the ancient Finns, who had used saunas for centuries as a place for purification, so he set about building a refuge where he could go and be one with his thoughts. Saunas date back centuries. Sometimes, old beer barrels were used; other times, small huts were constructed with a stove inside that was fed with wood and on which stones were placed. The smoke was released through a chimney or stack. The Finns would regularly strip down naked and sequester themselves inside for long periods of time, occasionally dousing the hot stones with water to create steam, which brought about heavy perspiration. The combination of the water being poured on the stones and the water pouring out of the body creates a balance and interchange that brings about a great sense of peace, of being centered. The sauna can be a great refuge from the ills of the world, a dark and quiet place to reflect, to pray for others, and to heal.

As Denny put together his design, the materials to complete the project just seemed to show up—from the heavy piping needed for the stove to the large glass block that would form a cross in the side of the sauna, a block which just "happened" to be sitting around in his father-in-law's garage waiting to be noticed. Just short of the one-year anniversary of Tim's death, a "holy place" had been constructed near the tree line in the Wotchko side yard. It is a splendid structure, and you can feel the good energy Denny has put into each and every nail and molding. A call was made to christen the little cathedral, and on a Wednesday night in early 2003, Denny and I, along with Chelsey's dad Doug and Duane Kinnart, made our way into the little hot house for a good cleansing.

Candles lit the changing area as the fire inside the stove illuminated the entire interior and threw a reddish-yellow light through the glass blocks onto the snow outside in the shape of a cross. We made our way into the sitting area, closed the door behind us, and waited in the silence. Dennis poured water onto the super-heated rocks, and the combination of wood, metal, and stone created nothing short of a womb of sorts. I still get that feeling every single time I step into that holy place—the process of letting go and being reborn many times over. I do not exactly recall the conversation that first night. More than likely, there was not much talking but a lot of listening to within. After a couple hours of roasting ourselves, we sat outside in the cold night air and felt like new men. The pain, suffering, and anguish that one builds up began to lose their grip on our souls.

We began to converge every Wednesday, and soon "The Buffalo," our friend Dave who is a seeker and master woodcarver, joined us. His nickname fits. A robust figure with a jutting beard and broad back, Dave lived in downstate Michigan but would join us when he was visiting. There we would sit, five of us huddled naked in the searing heat. With four of us being two hundred pounds or better, we were not left with a lot of room for anything but prayer—and pray we did. As the healing over the loss of his boy came to Dennis, our intentions began to focus on friends we knew and strangers we did not, for their health and healing, for their journeys. I would often think that five men, sitting without and going within, could generate at least some energy that might lessen someone's pain somewhere. Five fathers who once were boys and had gone through the grinder that life often can be became sort of a "holy quintet," with our focus divided into two parts. During the first half of a sauna, we would pray and focus on ourselves, the ways we had fallen down, and the ways we had risen up since our last roast fest. It was not quite like confession, but rather like a support group that kept each other in check. We knew that to be a positive influence in the world, we first had to make sure our own self was in order of high standing. During the second half of the sauna, someone's name would be brought up, and each of us would speak a little about that person, whether we knew him or not, and then would focus on whatever challenge this person was facing.

Time and time again, the wood was cut, the fire stoked, and the water poured on the stones. We never wanted to change the outcome, only to ask that the lesson be shown and learned, and that the truth, whatever it may be, be revealed. We did not want to play God but simply acknowledge that the Architect of the Universe had things in order, no matter how chaotic they may seem to the human mind. For just over three years, we met on Wednesday evenings at the Wotchko home and continued to cleanse ourselves of the rust that had built up since our last dousing and focus our attention on those who were in need of a little good energy. We prayed for and put thoughts to one man in particular for more than two years, and we simply held that the highest good came from his battle with cancer. I would speak these words into the darkness on his behalf: "My prayer is that Sam's body and all contained within were created by the infinite intelligence that lives within him and knows how to heal him. This healing presence is now transforming every atom of his being making him whole and perfect now and I give thanks for the perfection of this healing whatever route it may take." Sam recently passed away at the age of forty-nine. By speaking those words, my intent was not to prolong his life but rather recognize the life within him and to allow for whatever energy that could be transferred from me to him in that moment. Sam leaves behind a wife and thee daughters and now our focus shifts to their lives and journey without him, and for at least a few moments on a weekly basis, we "send" good thoughts and energy to another human being to simply recognize their efforts or challenge.

At some point, Doug Hewitt, Chelsey Jo's dad, began to think about his own sanctuary. While perusing the local bookstore for materials to build a pond, he came across a book on building a sauna using mortar and wood. He was intrigued by the short sentence that read, "If you can make mud pies and cut wood, you can build this sauna." He felt that he fit that category (although, truth is, the guy is extremely talented when it comes to building just about anything). Not one to spend much on himself, Doug thought about handing over the thirty-five bucks for the volume but decided against it. A few weeks later, he was sharing his thoughts on building a sauna and the book he came across with Dennis, who then proceeded to inform him that he had the very same book in the closet nearby. From that point on, as if in some unseen perfect order, every single bit of the "spirit house" came forth as needed.

I spent more than a few summers working with concrete when I was younger. Learning a trade like that never leaves you. I couldn't wait to be there when the cement mixer backed up in the Hewitt yard, and I really enjoyed contributing to the foundation of the sauna. Many hands played a role in the construction of the building, but it really was Doug's to build as he cut log after log and packed the walls with sawdust for insulation. He worked count-less hours creating a place that would be his to hole up in when the pain of losing a child was more than any parent could bear. When it was finished, the structure was nothing short of a masterpiece. Massive stones connected with mortar hold the walls together. The ample changing room leads into a two-tiered seating area inside the hot room and affords a place to stretch out if needed. This sauna is the polar opposite of Dennis's creation, which wraps you like a tight blanket and squeezes every last ounce of negativity from your system. Doug's sauna seems to infuse water into the body as opposed to sweating it out, even though sweating is putting it mildly. It soon became apparent that both ends of the spectrum were covered—one taking out what is needed and one replacing what has been lost.

I would be remiss not to mention the importance of water in all that occurs in the sauna. With our bodies being nearly 70 percent water, roughly the same percentage as the Earth, the constant movement in and out of the body brings a vitality and energy unlike anything I have ever experienced. As cold, clear water is poured slowly on the hot stones and magically turns to a mist that we inhale and that permeates the skin, it causes our inner water to mix with the outer. The same cycle that keeps the Earth alive is recreated for each of us. As I type these words, my backyard is filled with water—in its frozen form called snow and ice—but I know that, soon enough, it will melt and seep inward to the earth, bringing forth new life. Every moment I spend in the sauna gives me the opportunity to experience the very same thing. All the elements come into play—fire, water, air, and earth—restoring balance to the body and clarity to the mind.

It was not too long ago when it struck me that none of the things that had become so important to the five of us—time supporting each other, cleansing our minds and bodies, sitting in silence, regaining the energy to face the rat race for another week, or simply sitting in the cool night air with clouds of steam rising from our skin, not to mention the many people we had thought of and prayed for—none of it would exist had Chelsey and Tim still been alive. I began to think about the duality of what was going on—the loss and gain, the death and rebirth, the removal and infusing, and the ripple effect that had taken place, created from one moment frozen in time on a snowy February night.

This chapter was not part of the original lineup I had planned for inclusion in this book, but it seems the universe had other plans. It started with a wrong number and an automatic callback feature I did not know I had. In calling Duane last night, I mistakenly called Doug. There was no answer, so I hung up after six rings. Before I could try calling Duane again, the phone rang while still in my hand. It was Robin, Doug's wife, asking me why I had called. She explained that she had been talking with Kathy, Dennis's wife, when I had called. I told her of my misdial regarding Duane, and she informed me that the guys were going to do a sauna. It was the first time that Dennis had been able to make it in a long time. Since it was the day after Christmas, my naked buddies had figured I was still in Chicago and hadn't called me. Robin simply said, "I think you are supposed to be here."

So I postponed my writing appointment, headed the six miles to Doug's house, dropped my trousers, and found a familiar spot in the 180-degree heat, along with Dennis, Duane, Doug, and Dave. With four "Ds" and a "J," we might sound like some fifties doo-wop group, but the reality is that while all of us come from very different backgrounds and occupy different stations in life, we have one thing in common: our commitment to evolving from who we used to be to who we are capable of being, and then serving the world from a higher place than before. This was all made possible by two young people who, to the untrained mind, it may appear died too soon. Like all prophets and visionaries, it's more accurate to say they came in on time and left on time.

It had been well over a year since the five of us had all been in the same sauna at the same time. I thanked my friends for being such great teachers and leaders over the past five years. We talked for a long time about the massive growth that had taken place in our lives, and especially in Doug and Dennis's families, that perhaps might never have occurred without the death of their children. Make no mistake, grief is only a thought away, and for a greater portion of the past few years, anger and confusion over losing Chelsey and Tim have been a formidable foe. However, each of the fathers dealt with it in his own way and on his own time, and it truly has been a gift to watch each man overcome to some degree that which no parent can ever truly imagine: outliving your child. In one moment, their world changed. In another moment, they had a thought about building a place to heal that gave birth to moments for others to do the same.

Of course, the ultimate truth is that all of us are dying in our own way and time. We often refuse to acknowledge that death is part of the life cycle just because our picture isn't on the obituary page. This book is about moments that have made an impact on me, and as I write in the current moment, my thoughts turn to how important a few hours on a Wednesday evening have become. While the average American is watching television about four-and-a-half hours per night, we five are often inside the "spirit house" at the very same time, using our allotted moments to focus on ourselves and our fellow travelers on the life journey. Personally, I have never understood the concept of watching someone on television in produced "reality" while my "reality" goes slipping by unnoticed. If you create moments that challenge, uplift, and inspire, soon you won't have time to watch television. You will be too busy watching your life unfold in new and incredible ways.

For most of the week, these two structures sit dormant, waiting for someone to toss a few slabs of wood into the stove, open the damper, and strike a match, putting in motion a ritual so ancient that no one really knows when it began. Timeline not withstanding, our long-ago relatives knew that cleansing from the inside out was the way to go, and while our world is filled with stress and strain, surely theirs was too in its own way. Even when I am not "up north" on a Wednesday, I know that the others are in the sauna doing what they feel needs to be done and including me in the conversation. To make up for my absence, we usually do a Sunday night thing, but our tradition is on the day named after the god Woden.

Those who were lost, in fact, made possible the incredible healing of two families who lost a part of themselves. Out of the memory of Chelsey and Tim rose two small buildings that have housed a million good thoughts and twice as many prayers of thanks and blessing. Of course, the only thing "magical" about the saunas is what each of us brings to them every week and what we leave with after sweating out doubt, negativity, and pain. For me, that means no matter who you are or where you are, the opportunity exists to find a small, quiet spot where, on a weekly basis, you can forget who you used to be and remember who you can be. If it means building a sauna, so be it, but just like a church or any place of worship that is man-made, it's the intention of the blueprint that matters most.

Where two or three are gathered together in my name,
there am I in the midst of them.
—MATTHEW 18:20

14

No More Mr. Bad Guy

The Native American elder sat quietly by the fire. His young grandson had come to him and shared a dream he'd had that night. "Grandfather, I dreamt that there were two wolves inside me fighting for my attention. They were very hungry and wanted me to feed them. One was a black wolf that seemed to be filled with anger, envy, and rage. It snarled and snapped at me, trying to bite chunks of my flesh and eat away at me bit by bit."

"What of the other wolf?" asked the old man.

"The other wolf was pure white and seemed to be aglow with a bright light from within, filled with love, peace, and good things. It did not try to harm me, but rather sat nearby, waiting for me to invite it closer."

"And did you, my grandson?"

"Yes, Grandfather, but every time I did, the black wolf grew angry. It scared me, so I stopped. I am afraid, Grandfather. Which wolf will live inside me?"

The elder thought for a long moment and then said, "The one you feed the most."

The alchemists of old had one goal—transformation. They delved deep into the particles of perception and the concentration of matter in order to turn the ordinary into the extraordinary. They wanted to transform lead into gold, taking that which was of a lower vibration and value to something of a higher vibration and value. The concept of the alchemists is also the stuff of life, taking the heavy, leaden places inside us and, through the process of purification and melding of the soul to the higher self, transforming them into more than what we thought we could be. No one whom you might look up to today as a model of success or achievement came to this planet in his or her present form. Rather, they were forged from the fires of life—the ones that burn inside each one of us.

There are days when I really cannot believe the human race has "made it" as far as it has. Today, a nineteen-year-old shot up a mall, and eight people besides him will not see another birthday. A few days ago, a mother confessed that she had beaten her two-year-old to death with a cord and put the body in a plastic bin because the girl refused to go to sleep when ordered. Every day the news is filled with the lowest we can come up with as a species, and every horror story somehow takes a piece out of my soul. Truth is, we have been at each other since the beginning of time, and I suppose that depending on how you look at it, we have gotten better about killing each other off. Or maybe it's just that the ways we do it and the reasons we do it have changed. Or maybe not. For all the greatness we have inside us, there seems to be an equal measure of rage that some can control and others cannot. Surely, the fires of rage are fanned when the aforementioned offenses and a million just like them are brought to our attention, and maybe evolution is all about harnessing the rage and channeling the energy for a higher purpose. I know what that feels like.

I have no idea where my rage or anger came from, but they always seemed to be there. For most of my younger years, I walked the line between the higher and lower vibrations, my higher self soothed by music and nature and the lower self fueled by the contact that came with football.

Before I step any further, take note that football has been a great teacher for me and came with great teachers who instilled discipline, pride, and persistence in me, among other lessons. But the form of football, with all its drills and execution, came secondary to me in regard to the contact or pain that one can inflict within the legal bounds of the game. I was very good at the sport and played football as far back as I can remember. From playground pickup games to high school and college and then on to semi-pro, the gridiron seemed a place where I could release the beast within and not get arrested for trying to knock out some guy's teeth. I relished the defensive side of the ball, reacting to the offensive strategies and counteracting with as much force as possible.

As I went on in the game and grew stronger, my focus for most of the year was to be ready for football. I can remember spending hours in our basement after inhaling another meal, pounding weights into submission, surrounded by posters of L.A. Rams legend Deacon Jones, Chicago Bears icon Dick Butkus, and bodybuilder Lou Ferrigno. I wanted to be bigger and badder than anyone on the field, and by the time I was in college, I had sculpted a six-foot-two, 215-pound, rock-hard physique.

After three seasons and a four-year stint in the service, my weight training had added another twenty pounds to my frame. The amount of metal I could push had jumped from a bench press of 350 pounds to 475 pounds, which gave me the ability to do "negatives" (an exercise in which you lower the weight on the bench press and a partner helps you raise it back to the start position) with a total of 605 pounds. I had pushed my body to the maximum, but not all of it was natural.

While in the service, a guy I was stationed with entered a bodybuilding contest, and I trained alongside him with no intention of entering myself. Somewhere along the line, he admitted he was using steroids, administered to him by his girlfriend who was a nurse. He invited me to try them, and being the invincible twenty-something I was, I agreed. I don't remember the exact drug or injection schedule, but I do recall dropping my shorts for a shot in the hip for five months or so. Ironically, the guy dropped out of the training, and I went on to compete in the Mr. Illinois contest and did pretty well. Interestingly, I don't think there was a huge increase in how I looked, but there was a definite change in how I felt.

When you are larger than the average Joe on the street and have a growing chip on your shoulder, the only way you can maintain that stance is to reinforce it through some sort of violent behavior. You walk around with a sort of armor on, always ready to defend who you are and the identity you have created. I used to joke that when I came down the street, people would walk across the road to avoid me. It was funny back then, but sad when I look at it now. As I struggled to find my way in the world, knowing that the NFL was never going to call, my anger grew and the outlet for the beast shrank. I played semi-pro until I was nearly thirty years old, and now I realize that the game was secondary to the need I had to inflict pain if at all possible. I had the act down pat, of course—closely shaved head most of the time, a scowl that made me look like the bad ass I hoped everyone saw in me. It got difficult trying to hold up that persona all the time and even more difficult to validate the pain I could cause. There are two incidents that stick in my mind.

Being a bouncer at a bar was the perfect part-time job for me. For a year or two, I patrolled a Chicago establishment on the northwest side of town, along with my pal Bubba. We were the perfect combination of Thunder and Lightning. Bubba was a six-foot-three, 350-pound behemoth who stood guard at the door like a great redwood tree. I would usually patrol inside the bar, and then we would switch off for a change of scenery. The lights would come on for last call, and more times than not we were making sure that the drunkards were escorted off the premises in a timely fashion. There is nothing like having some guy who weighs 150 pounds soaking wet get in your face after a night of quarter beers. The lower levels of liquid courage always had something going on, and to this day I really don't like to frequent a bar atmosphere. When you see a man's head bounced off the side of a pool table, it tends to dampen the celebration.

One night, some guy had had more than enough, and he started to drool over one of the regular girls who showed up on Friday nights. I let it go for a long time and then finally asked him to leave. He, of course, promptly told me where to go. He was a biker with a cutoff jean vest and insignia on the back. I stood next to him, waiting for him to leave, and finally had to get between him and the girl. He then decided to stab his finger into my chest, which gave me cause to grab him by the hair, spin him around, and run him out the door. One thing about drunks in bars and bouncers—it's never going to be an even match. The drunk is, well, drunk, and the bouncers are not, and for the most part the bouncers were picked because they could handle themselves and a few others without blinking an eye.

I walked the guy toward his motorcycle and promptly stepped back to avoid any more confrontation. He decided that he wanted to continue our relationship and took a swing that caught me flush on the side of the head. I saw stars that triggered the anger in me that was always at a slow burn, now bursting fully into rage. I hit him once between the eyes and swept his feet out from under him. While he was falling, I caught him under the shoulders and made sure that his landing pad was the big, knuckled bolt that was sticking out of the top of the fire hydrant next to his bike. As his lower back struck the iron, he let out a loud groan, and I proceeded to put one hand across his chest and my other hand near his stomach. I pushed down with all the force I had, intent on impaling this punk. He had bitten off more than he could chew, I thought. His mind was trying to write checks his body couldn't cash, and I was going to prove it.

I'm not sure how long I was holding him down before a few guys from the bar pulled me off the man. I hesitate to think where I would be today if the bar patrons had not stopped me, for my goal was to break him in half. He had staggered to his feet by the time the cops arrived, and I was told to make myself scarce. I never heard anything about his whereabouts or condition after that. I had no remorse about my actions at the time. I felt justified in doing my job and that somehow the guy deserved it after running into the likes of me. But it was only a few weeks later that another incident became the catalyst for moving me in a new direction.

It was a late summer evening, and I cannot recall the exact circumstances that led to the fight on the street in front of the bar. I clearly remember sitting on the hood of a car, with my arms locked around a guy's neck, his head tilted to one side while I cut off the blood to his brain in a "sleeper hold" that would render him unconscious. I was also twisting his head from side to side, and he was choking violently. Even though Bubba was busy breaking up another part of the brawl, the guy's bulging eyes told the story. The big man came over and grabbed my arms to pry them open, but I would not budge. He talked me into letting go while exerting a constant pressure, enough to help the guy breathe and finally slip to the ground. I came back to reality to find that a crowd had gathered to watch the show. The guy I had been strangling was helped to his feet. His name was Brian, and he was someone I knew from the bar. He had never given me trouble before and even played softball with us. Without Bubba's intervention, there is no telling how far I would have gone. In the dark, I hadn't recognized someone whom I knew as a "friendly." This time when I went home, the voice inside me was not one of validation but rather crucifixion. I could have killed someone for no reason. I was tired of being someone who instilled fear instead of faith, pain instead of possibility. It was time for a change.

A few weeks later, someone told me about "EST" or Erhard Seminar Trainings, named after Werner Erhard, a self-help pioneer from the 1970s. I attended a preliminary event, decided to attend the training, and came up with the 250 bucks. I jumped headlong into the training that would be held over two weekends with an evening in between. Of course, I attended in full battle armor, with my head in a buzz cut, clad in jeans and a leather jacket that I wore all day during the training. Keeping in line with the covenant of not revealing what happens in the seminars, I will not go into any specifics, but I did witness amazing acts of courage and truth from the people who attended. The observations and insights were coming fast and furious, and I started to unload some major baggage. But it wasn't until a few hours before the seminar ended that the wheels really came off for me.

I had been sitting for a few hours listening to the instructor when I began to notice that the guy in the row in front of me and to my right was nodding off to sleep. I watched with growing annoyance at this man not paying attention (in my book) and dismissing what was being offered. *How dare he sleep in a seminar I had paid for!* My anger grew as none of the assistants in the room moved to wake him up. I let it go for as long as I could, and then in one reactionary moment, I pulled back my leg and kicked him right out of the chair and onto the floor. *He's awake now,* I thought. The seminar assistants rushed over to the scene as a couple of hundred heads turned to watch. "If you assholes were doing your job, I wouldn't have had to wake up this jerk," I growled. The man was still wondering what hit had him, and I was vehemently defending my right to kick ass any time I saw fit. They moved him to another chair, and I felt validated in my life-long stance as the harbinger of right and wrong. Feeling well satisfied in my rightness, I settled into my chair as the seminar resumed and . . . promptly fell asleep myself.

Retribution was swift as the woman sitting next to me swung her very pointed elbow right into my ribs, waking me up and knocking the wind out of me. I doubled over in pain and fell to my knees on the carpet. I sat there gasping for air and recovered to come face-to-face with my adversary: a slight, dark-haired woman named Sue. The assistants rushed back, of course, but this time I got it. The armor was rusting off, and it was the beginning of the end for Mr. Bad Guy. Later that evening when the seminar ended, I gave Sue my leather coat as a souvenir. She and I became friends and stayed in touch for many years.

The process of becoming a better being and a greater human had been engaged, and over the past twenty-five years I have made it my business to give rather than take, to add to and not subtract from, to build up rather than tear down, whenever and wherever I can. That one decision to immerse myself in what is possible with regard to leaving the lower part of me behind has put me on a lifelong adventure to the farthest reaches of the most important universe known to humankind . . . the universe within.

There are times when I still feel that burn inside, but it's usually as a result of something I have seen on the news rather than from standing guard at the door. Even the transcribing of this chapter brought back to me the vivid feelings and thoughts I had when I was a different person. I relived my sadness at hurting Brian that night, and the total embarrassment of falling asleep in my chair at

EST and getting knocked to my knees by a woman half my size. As I look back on these few incidents, I am reminded that growth is a process that does not happen overnight. In getting back to the core of who we are, our lives demand that we work backward through the experiences we have built up, layer after layer, much like the growth rings in a tree. I've also learned that it was my perception of what was going on, not the actual events themselves, that fed the rage inside me. I had to see through my blinders in order to make a change and get about the business of living.

With an average of just about 28,000 days for the average American life span, spending an inordinate amount of that allotted time being angry, upset, pissed off, or filled with rage seems to diminish the gift of life. As I have channeled my energy into more useful and beneficial activities, my life has responded in kind. I no longer see the world as a place that I have to be on guard against, but rather as a place for which to be grateful. The rage has been transformed into redemption, and it serves to keep me alert and filled with the notion that the ancient alchemists had it right. The only way to transform one metal into another is through a process that strips away all that is no longer needed and rearrange what's left into a shining, precious thing.

As a side note to this chapter, I felt it was important to include moments that shaped me, even though at the time they would not be considered "spiritual" or "warm and fuzzy." Some of life's greatest opportunities for growth and change come during times of our deepest sorrows and lowest actions. The opposites in our internal horizons give us perspective and the ability to see where we have been. No doubt, my actions were those of a lower thought and vibration, but if they gave birth to the man I am becoming, then they served their purpose. We cannot get the full measure of good without knowing the bad in depth. Yes, I am convinced that all that evil needs to thrive in this world is for good people to do nothing. But I am also convinced that evil is a great opportunity to know grace and goodness as part of life. It is, in fact, a call to action. Without one, we would not know the other, and being a part of both gives one the chance to choose which master to serve.

You will not be punished for your anger;
you will be punished by your anger.
—BUDDHA (568–488 BC)

15

No Parking

We live in a world filled with signs that are posted for one reason only: to inform us. All kinds of signs tell us what direction to take, where to find food, which place has the lowest prices, what to do in an emergency, how fast to drive, and, of course, where *not* to park. But, really, who ever pays attention to signs? We drive over the limit, still have to ask for directions, and, for the most part, ignore signs, no matter where they are posted or how big they are. If you have ever felt like "the system" was out to get you, and then the system hauled your butt out of look-what-happened-to-me land, then this chapter on ignoring signs and then looking for them is right up your billboard.

It started out like any other hot, humid, melt-your-bones July day in Chicago. I had a full day of radio lined up. For the most part, it was going really well, so by noon when it was time to put on the feedbag, I decided to be a most gracious boss and take my team out to lunch for one of the Windy City's most sought-after food items: hot dogs.

Before I go any further, let me state for the record that while I am fully aware of the horror stories that abound about how hot dogs are made and what goes into them, let me be frank (sorry) and say that I don't care. Some might say they will contribute in part to my eventual demise, but I don't smoke, rarely drink, and always wear a seat belt—so there. I will also state in print, as a bona fide Chicagoan, that we have better dogs than any other city, whether you consume them at the world-famous Superdawg under the watchful eyes of "Flaurie and Maurie," the twelve-foot-tall statues of a male and female hot dog, or at Roma's Italian Beef & Sausage, where you could get drawn and quartered if you ask for ketchup on the dog, or at Portillo's, which has been part of the Chicago landscape since 1963 when Dick Portillo opened up a dog stand in a trailer and now boasts more than forty-five locations. Any way you slice it, Chicago is home of the best hot dogs on planet Earth.

So it was off to Portillo's for some dogs with all the trimmings with my team. (The cheeseburgers and beef sandwiches are just as amazing, with the latter served juicy with extra sweet peppers.) The windows were down, and we were talking about radio stuff and playing some good tunes to round out the ride. What could possibly go wrong?

Chicago is an amazing city, but sometimes the way it's laid out leaves a little to be desired when it comes to parking, particularly where and for how long. There is a bit of "brother-in-law" going on . . . that is, if it is lunchtime and you are only going to be in a spot for a short time, it's no big deal. The cops leave you alone because everyone is out for the same thing: chow. You don't want to make a career out of sitting in a parking spot, but everyone knows what everyone is up to from noon to one or so.

The drive-thru window was backed up, so I did what every other red-blooded Chicagoan would do: found a spot in a lot that would not be in anyone's way, but close enough so that we did not have to find a cab to get back to the restaurant. Right across the street from my destination was a drugstore, part of a major chain that you would know, but for reasons of literary safety I'll just call the "Big Drug Store." So I made a split-second decision upon seeing the lineup waiting for food and swung into the parking lot of the Big Drug Store and found a spot in the middle of the lot, which had just a few cars in it. As I pulled in to the first slot that appealed to me, I looked up to see a very large sign that read: NO PARKING. VIOLATORS WILL BE TOWED AT OWNER EXPENSE.

While a small tinge of "what if" ran through my mind, I did what anyone else would do: I ignored the sign. However, so that I would not take up an "important" spot, I moved the car to the farthest spot in the lot, one engulfed in a large pool of muddy water. Secure in the knowledge that humans have been ignoring no-parking signs since they've been posting them, my team and I went off to gorge on hot dogs.

The wait, of course, took longer than usual, and twice I looked over to make sure that my newly purchased Aurora was still in its stall. When the meal was finished and the table cleared, we headed across the street into the bright summer sun, my keys in hand. But when we reached the parking spot, nothing remained but a few pigeons taking a bath in the filthy water where my car once stood.

At first, I stared in disbelief. It really did not sink in that the car was not there. I didn't have the nerve to turn around and look at my team because the look on my face was not something I wanted to share at that moment. Then I grew indignant. Tow *my* car? The outrage! #&$%)#&@)@%!& Then came the sinking feeling . . . the sloped shoulders and the "Holy crap, what now?" I looked at the big sign that now said: DO NOT PARK HERE BECAUSE IF YOU DO THEN YOU ARE GOING TO HAVE TO PAY IN MORE WAYS THAN ONE. YOU ARE GOING TO LOOK STUPID, FEEL BAD, AND HAVE A ROTTEN AFTERNOON ALL BECAUSE YOU THOUGHT THE SIGN DID NOT

APPLY TO YOU! Nice. While it was possible that someone had stolen my ride, a sick feeling in my stomach told me that the wrecker got it. The sign had the address of the auto pound clearly posted, and I knew the longer it sat there, the more money it was going to cost me.

It was time to fly into action. I told the team to grab a cab back to the office, and I would meet them back there when I retrieved the car. I turned down their offer to cab it back and then have one of them drive me to pick up the car. I knew that would take more time and I needed to gather my thoughts. So, off they went in one direction, while I hailed another cab that stopped, turned right at the corner, and pulled directly into a gas station when I told the driver the address I was headed to.

"I don't have enough gas to get that far," he told me.

"How far is it?" I grumbled.

"More than forty blocks, sir."

So I jumped out of that cab and grabbed a fully fueled one. The driver took off down the pothole-laden path toward my car, which in my mind had now been dropped off at a junkyard amidst a pile of rusted metal hulks and other city dwellers waiting in line for a chance to explain their stupidity.

When you have time to sit (for more than forty blocks in mid-day Chicago traffic), your mind begins to work on you. That little voice (not the still, small voice, but the I-told-you-so voice) gnaws on your central nervous system like a blunt chain saw hacking on a stump. *Should have gone in the drive-thru . . . should have called ahead . . . should have stayed in bed . . . should be a vegan . . .* By the time I pulled up at the compound, I had little mental gas of my own left. I thanked the driver, got out of the car, and waited at the window of a building that looked like a cross between the San Quentin lockup and a rural gas station. When the attendant came and confirmed that the car was there, I turned to the cabbie, gave him a thumbs-up, and off he went. I paid the $200 bill for towing while trying to explain to the guy behind the bulletproof glass how the world had done me wrong. He just nodded because he had heard it all a thousand times before. Slowly, the side gate slid back like I was about to walk the Green Mile. As I made my way to my car through the sunbaked gravel with the rays of sunshine glaring angrily off metal, I kept thinking that all I had wanted that day was a hot dog. I got one all right, but it just cost me a couple hundred dollars.

Finally, I found my car. I rested for a moment on the shady side and breathed a sigh of relief that, while the day did not go as I had hoped, I would soon be back in the air-conditioned comfort of my ride and in the flow of work in no time. I dug in my pocket . . . then the other pocket . . . then the back pockets . . . NO KEYS. My mind flashed back to the cab ride . . . one cab to another. Where were they? I raised my voice to the heavens and cried out loud, "ARE YOU FRIGGING KIDDING ME?" The gnawing chain saw voice in my brain started up again. *Maybe you should have obeyed the sign and parked somewhere else . . .*"

Shut up, I thought, just shut up.

Okay, so the keys were gone, but since I had broken this, I could fix it! Down but not out, I quickly called my former brother-in-law, Joe, who is the world's greatest locksmith. He would know what to do. He could just make me a key and some-how get it to me. Unfortunately, Joe was less optimistic. Something about VIN numbers and microchips in the ignition key and the codes being in Seattle . . . and if he could pull it off, it might take, hmmm, about four hours! In four hours, I would be baked to a crisp like a roadkill horned toad in the summer heat, not to mention insane from the thoughts in my head that kept pounding away. *Shouldn't have parked there . . .* Grrrrrr.

But Joe said he would check into it, so I began to feel that the situation was now beyond my control. As if to drive the point right into the ground, a tow truck came in with another victim attached to the back, dropped off the car, and then pulled up next to where I was standing. The driver rolled down the window and said, "What the hell are you just standing here for?" I told him about the keys, to which he replied, "You're up shit creek, huh?" Adding insult to injury, he then reminded me not to wander around the junkyard because the security cameras were on, and if anything looked suspicious, the six rabid dogs on the property would take a chunk out of my ass.

Great. Not only was I stranded in a junkyard, but also I couldn't even move to shade without having a dog pack dismember me—all because I did not obey a clearly posted sign. No matter how I tried to turn it, make it fit, or pass the buck, the fact was that I had made the choice to park where I shouldn't have. I had ignored the sign, and now I was paying for it. There was only one thing left to do.

I stood on the bleached gravel amidst the seared metal of the cars and declared out loud to the universe, "I messed up! I am totally responsible for parking where I shouldn't have. I know there is a greater lesson in this for me, like ignoring all the other signs in my life that would have made the journey a bit less difficult if I would just really listen within. I cannot fix this on my own, and I need help to restore this situation to a place that I can learn from and move from in a good way. At this moment, I surrender the outcome and get out of the way. Thank you for bringing my keys back to me so I can get back to work and out of the heat."

As soon as I said those words, my shoulders relaxed and my mind let go. I began to notice the blue of the summer sky, the green of the trees outside the fence, and the determination of the weeds growing through the gravel. The sun, while still very hot, made me feel alive, as if it had just risen a moment ago. A big grin broke across my face, and I began to laugh out loud. *Got me again, God,* I thought. *Good one.*

Not more than two minutes later, my cellphone rang, and it was my office on the line. I had called them with the little bit of battery I had left on my cell to put out an alert for my keys (and let them know not to expect me anytime soon . . .). They had contacted the major cab companies in Chicago and put out the word that a set of keys was missing. By chance (uh-huh), the cabbie that had dropped me off had pulled into the garage to check the air pressure in his tire and noticed a set of keys on the backseat. Right about that time, the announcement came over the loudspeaker about my predicament. The cabbie called in that he was returning to the junkyard, and the cab company called my office, which called me. All this happened in the very moment when I was "letting go." I hung up the phone, bent over, and touched the ground in a gesture of thanks. Once again, I knew that the whole thing had been a divine setup from the get-go, and in the end, the only way I could "fix it" was by letting go and letting Spirit handle the details.

I made my way to the junkyard office where, by now, my little circus act and I were the center of attention. I boldly stepped into the office, looked my jailers right in the eyes, and said, "There are 13,000 cabs in Chicago, but I only needed one to hear me, and he is on his way back with my keys!" There were high-fives all around, and something told me that these hard-bitten junkyard guys needed a win that day, too.

The cabbie came zooming up the street with his window down and a huge smile on his face, waving my keys in celebration. He pulled a U-turn and parked by the curb. I knelt in the open door and thanked him profusely. He said, "I am not sure why I went back to the garage. I was done for the day and had turned off my radio, so I never heard the bulletin about your missing keys." I felt horrible because I had spent all my cash on hot dogs and was down to a credit card for a reward. He refused to tell me his name (and when I called the cab company later, they were not sure who he was). He simply smiled and said, "God bless you," and then drove away. Not wanting to waste one more minute, I ran back to my car, fired it up, put down the windows to exhaust the hot air, and drove back to my desk with a feeling of being looked after that has never fully left me. When I got back to the office, I related the story to the staff, and it was no longer the topic of discussion by the end of the day.

This adventure is a running joke now whenever the subject of hot dogs comes up. But while I laugh it off, all I have to do is close my eyes to once again feel the sun on my face, the heat that rose up from the twisted metal around me, the dust kicked up by the truck driver, and the deep sense of frustration I felt because I did not heed a warning . . . a sign. I can also recall in vivid detail the feeling I had when I let it all go and detached from the outcome. If that meant I had to wait four hours for a locksmith in Seattle to find my chip or set up camp with the rabid dogs in the junkyard, so be it. In a moment of surrender, the answer appeared, as it always does.

Signs are everywhere in our lives. We miss most of them because we are too busy. But there are also those that are clearly posted—those that we actually see, but often ignore—and, in the end, that is probably our biggest folly as a species. Nixon announced in 1973 that we were far too dependent on foreign oil, and still we act surprised when prices go through the roof. Financial cutbacks for after-school programs put kids on the streets, and we wonder why crime goes up. We glorify athletes, actors, and others who act irresponsibly, and then wonder why our kids do the same thing. We park in places we shouldn't because we feel that the sign must apply to someone else, when signs do, in fact, apply to all of us. Don't believe me? Next time you are in Chicago and hungry for a hot dog from Portillo's, park across the street in the Big Drug Store lot and see what happens. Remember, it's a forty-block ride.

In complex trains of thought, signs are indispensable.
—GEORGE H. LEWES (1817–1878)

16

The Sack Man

Once upon a time, a man decided that, for at least one night, he was going to fill some mighty big boots. He had just the right red suit with the fur trimmings, the hat that hung to one side with a bright fur ball on the end and a clip of holly just above the left ear, an ample belt that would fit around a couple of pillows, and suspenders to hold the rig in place. His trousers were tucked neatly into the almost-knee-high boots, and his face, of course, had the perfect flowing beard that was covered at the ears with curls of white that sprouted from under his hat. His eyes were set under white bushy eyebrows and shone a bright blue from behind the small, wire-rimmed glasses. Even his hands reflected the outfit, encased in white gloves with a small bracelet of bells on one wrist that jingled just right. What the man did not know was that his willingness to make sure that a few kids smiled on Christmas Eve would turn into fifteen years of giving and receiving, laughter and tears, and an amazing moment just when he needed it most.

I had been in the Coast Guard just over six months and was stationed at the NAS Glenview, Illinois. Two HH52A choppers were in the hangar, and an attachment of about sixty "coasties" was responsible for everything in the water and on land south of a line from Chicago that divided Lake Michigan in half across to Grand Haven, Michigan. Being just out of boot camp, I was a Seaman First Class, robust and steadfast in my military bearing and eager to make my time in the service count for something. My lieutenant was a great guy named Rusty Munsey, and it was an incredible time of growth for me, being around pilots and Guard veterans. I was one marching-in-step lifer, and when I look at pictures of myself from back then, with the military haircut, square jaw, and blue uniform, there is no way to tell that I would wear another uniform far longer than my government issue.

Christmas 1980 was fast approaching, and at some point, a volunteer was needed for an on-base party that was being held for the kids of the approximately five hundred Air Force, Army, Marines, Coast Guard, and Navy personnel attached to the naval air station. Before I knew what I was volunteering for, my hand went up. Being the eager young boy in blue that I was, I soon reported to the captain's office for my mission. It was a short meeting and right to the point. "Seaman, you will be the Santa Claus at the base children's party, and then you will also do the same at our own Coast Guard party that evening. Thank you for volunteering, and I expect you to serve with pride behind that beard. That is all." I saluted, spun on my heels, and exited his office. It only took about a minute to realize that I had been set up. It turned out that it was the Guard's year to furnish a Santa. No one else wanted to do it, and it was agreed by all that when the volunteer question came up, no other hands would be raised. I was a predetermined Kris Kringle, like it or not.

A day or two later, the base outfit arrived in a box, and upon inspection I knew that some surgery was in order to save its life. The suit was well worn and threadbare in spots, and the hair and beard looked like something the cat had dragged in. The beard, in particular, was nasty, and I could just imagine some old, snuff-chewing salt spitting through the acrylic hair. I did what any self-respecting Santa-in-training would do—I called my mom, gave her the lowdown, and talked her into doing some serious suit upgrades in the name of serving her country. In the meantime, I went on the hunt for a beard and hair rig. Within a week, what once was a large red rag in the making had become a work of art due to Mom's holiday spirit and sewing prowess. I donned the entire outfit and checked myself in the full-length mirror at my folks' house. The transformation was incredible.

With my new duds, I took center stage at the base party, holding court from a very large chair in the auditorium while hundreds of kids lined up to tell me what was on their wish list. This was long before video games or personal computers or cellphones or any of the other electronic flotsam that floods the markets today. I was asked for teddy bears, Barbies, bicycles, dollhouses, and GI Joes. As the night went on, I began to look forward to each child hopping up on my lap and telling me things about their lives that I was sure their parents did not know. After four straight hours of kids and their dreams, the evening finally came to an end.

I went back to the hangar and got ready to skin out of my suit and take a long, hot shower, but when I went into the empty locker room, I caught a glimpse of myself in the mirror. My hat was crooked, and there were a few stains on the front of my jacket. My beard was stuck with peppermint (from the kids) and coffee (from me). I felt like I had gone a few rounds with the champ, but I also had a sense of elation. For a few hours, Santa Claus and I got to share a spirit and make a difference in the lives of little kids. I showed up at the Guard Christmas party and received a nice round of applause and a cold beer (and other holiday spirits) for my efforts.

That one Santa stint grew into a yearly excursion during my enlistment. I went to kids' homes off base, often at the request of military officers, and did a couple more "evenings with Santa." When I was honorably discharged after four years, my service to the country ended, but my service to Christmas was just beginning. I eventually bought a really good Santa suit—a corduroy deal that was top of the line. I splurged on a beard and wig that looked like the real thing and dug up a pair of my grandmother's granny glasses to round out the look. I started sitting in at a friend's floral shop a few weeks before Christmas and accepted invites from parents who wanted a "real Santa" to show up.

The routine was pretty simple. I would arrive at the designated place and time, find the sack of goodies that had been hidden, knock on the door, and make a grand entrance. The reaction from children was somewhat predictable, but it was the adults—who did not know who I was—that really got me going. Sometimes the parents left a note with names for me to throw out while doling out the presents, and I am here to say that watching someone's Uncle Dan scratch his head and wonder how the heck I knew him was worth the drive every time. My visits would last about ten minutes, and off I would go in my Golden Eagle Jeep CJ5 loaded for the next stop. I buzzed through the streets of Chicago in full regalia, the door of my Jeep open and my beard flying in the wind. It was a grand time.

Over the years, the list of homes got longer, the breakfasts with Santa got more crowded, and my annual excursion on Christmas Eve would often carry over to Christmas Day as I did my best to make the rounds. I could fill volumes from the memories of my yearly excursions, like the time I stopped at the bank to make a withdrawal and was escorted in and out by the security guards who were more than a little suspicious about my outfit. Then, of course, there was the time that I scaled the two-story back porch at the house next door to my in-laws and surprised the family by coming in the patio window and not the front door. One time, I stopped at the home of a friend who had a little girl, only to find that I was the first English-speaking Santa she had ever seen. Her whole family spoke Polish. There were countless stops and gifts, more smiles from strangers than you could ever count, and endless lines of children at churches and schools waiting for their turn with the right, jolly, old elf.

There was one family that I stopped in to see for about eight years in a row. Their house was spectacularly decorated, and it was a thrill to watch their daughter grow from age five to thirteen and be a part of their family celebration. I really looked forward to seeing the parents and grandparents, who were thrilled at my yearly appointment. One thing that never changed was the little hairless dog that sat snarling on Grandma's lap, his sole Christmas wish being to tear out the seat of my pants.

As my kids were born and grew older, my last stop of the night was at home, long after they had gone to bed. I would sneak up the stairs, smelling of night air, cookies, and snow, and slowly creep into their room with the sound of bells jingling. They would wake up, sleepy-eyed and warm, as I sat on their beds and recited *The Night before Christmas.* When I finished, I would give them a big hug and say good night. I relish those nights that seem so very long ago, mostly because I knew they would end . . . and end they did, now that my kids are twenty and seventeen.

In 1995, I had been donning the red suit with all the trimmings for fifteen years, and it was getting more difficult to be away on Christmas Eve as my own kids enjoyed the magic of the season. As the holiday approached, I felt that perhaps this would be the year that I stopped and stayed home. This would be the year that I did not see the snarling dog and the girl whose house was a showcase. This would be the year that someone else would do "Breakfast with Santa." And this would be the year that I put the beard and glasses away for good.

I told no one about my plans, but as we prepared to head out to visit with the in-laws for the evening, I finally broke down and told my wife that Santa was grounded for good. She was more than surprised, but out of habit and as a back-up measure, I threw the suit in the trunk of the car. We headed out over the river and through the woods and enjoyed a wonderful evening. As the time drew near for me to make my usual exit to don my Santa attire, I announced to the adults that I would be staying put and that another hot toddy was in order. I laughed about it with the others, but it bothered me deeply that a tradition I had held sacred for so long had come to an end. My prayer was that someone else would hear the jingle of the bells and take my place. That would be the best Christmas gift ever.

We sat for a long time around the tree and caught up on the latest in life and the kids, indulging in goodies and drink. I was so very glad to be a part of just spending time with loved ones, but I was also still feeling deeply torn about my decision to stay out of chimneys when the front doorbell rang. My father-in-law answered, and there in the doorway stood Santa! His suit was a bit on the bargain-rack side and his beard seemed to be more cotton balls than hair, but, hey, the guy was giving an earnest effort, and it was as if my prayers had been answered in record time. It took about a minute to figure out that "Santa" was Craig, the next-door neighbor, and he might have been dipping into the holiday punch a little too long. Either way, it was good to see him wishing us a happy holiday, and it felt like my wish came true to some extent.

After his exit, the talk, of course, turned back to my decision, and the gathered were sure that I had alerted Craig and put him up to the appearance, which I had not. But I did feel much better about the evening and thought that after a nightcap I would send myself off to the land of nod along with the kids. As the clock neared midnight and the fire was waning, a silence came over the few of us who were still awake. The tree was warmly lit, and presents littered the floor ready for the morning rush. A light snow was falling, and it was one of those precious slices of time when it feels like you have stepped into a Norman Rockwell painting. The spirit of Christmas enveloped us.

Suddenly, I heard another knock on the door. Great-Grandmother Alice was first to the door, and I expected another visit from Santa Craig. She opened up, and I can still see her take a step back with a look of amazement on her face. She turned to all of us in the room and said, "John . . . it's for you." I slowly rose from my chair and made my way to the foyer. Looking out the doorway, there on the stoop was . . . umm . . . Santa Claus! He was dressed in black trousers that were held up with thick suspenders and wore shiny black boots. His ample belly was covered with a red and white plaid shirt, and his magnificent beard reached mid-chest. The mass of white hair on his head touched his shoulders, and he had a small brown pipe in his mouth. His face was crinkled into a smile. He reached out his hand and simply said, "Merry Christmas, John."

With my mouth hanging open and a crowd of onlookers gawking out the windows, I extended my hand to him. He said, "I just wanted to thank you for everything you've done." We shook hands there on the stoop, with a light snow cascading down, and in that moment fifteen years of giving came back to me in the most amazing way. "I'm off!" he yelled, and jumped into the limo that was parked farther down the driveway. I had not moved from the spot where we had met, and I didn't know what to say or how to react.

Now it was my turn for conspiracy theories. Did my father-in-law pull off a good one? I grilled him hard, but he said no. The fact that no one except my wife knew that I would be staying at the house that night narrowed down the suspects to one. Was she behind it? Another resounding no. So what had happened? Who was this guy, and where did he come from? Why show up right at midnight, and how did he know my name was John? My analytical mind was lit up like a Christmas tree, and it was Great-Grandmother Alice who simply said, "Maybe it *was* Santa."

I relented, for what I had asked for, prayed for, and hoped for had been shown to me not once, but twice. Matter of fact, it was a reflection of my tenure as Kris Kringle, starting out with a threadbare suit and ending with a classical representation of Father Christmas. I lay awake most of the night, no longer in analysis but rather wonder, having been touched at my core by the image of the man in red. I wondered if that's how the endless number of children and scores of adults felt after I had stopped to shake a hand, give a hug, or roll out a hearty "Merry Christmas to all and to all a good night. . . ."

It's just a few weeks before Christmas, and I purposely put off writing this chapter until the tree was up, the lights were lit, and the stockings were hung by the chimney with care. Twenty-eight years ago, I raised my hand to volunteer for what I thought was a simple mission—to "play" Santa for some kids for a few hours. What was in store for me was a far greater mission to, in some small way, hold the space for one of the true meanings of Christmas—giving. Not the giving of gifts that are on a list or in the sale paper or paraded across the television, but rather the giving of our lives to something greater than our immediate wants and needs. The giving of oneself to another, and especially to a child, that potent nucleus who is one day going to be an adult.

While it's true that Santa Claus has become a Madison Avenue pitchman, it's also true that the origins of St. Nicholas are as pure as the driven snow, and that was the man I intended to emulate year after year. Stepping into his boots, and simply wanting to make children smile and adults remember the wonder of being alive, is of the highest calling. Every year on Christmas Eve, I take a few moments to think about all those kids who sat on my lap, told me their most sacred secrets, and said they loved me. Many were dirt-poor or sick, some were even dying, but for a few moments none of that mattered. What shone through is another true meaning of Christmas—love for one another.

About six months after Santa showed up at my in-laws' house, rumor was that the guy in the limo was in fact looking for someone named John but had gotten lost and stopped at the wrong house. I prefer to believe that, whether he knew it or not, his directions were perfect. He stopped at the right house and right on time.

There are three stages of a man's life: He believes in Santa Claus; he doesn't believe in Santa Claus; he is Santa Claus.
—AUTHOR UNKNOWN

17

Turtle Crossing

You can see the sign on just about every major freeway—you know, that big one that says "WRONG WAY DO NOT ENTER" and is posted for those hardy souls attempting to enter the lanes from an off ramp, not an on ramp. It's a clear warning that if you continue on the same route, it's going to hurt—a lot—and you might not be the only one who pays the price for going the wrong way. Life, however, while often like a highway, usually does not give such clear signs. We may wander for years down the same old paths, worn thin by our addictions, dramas, and lies. But since they are comfortable (albeit miserable), we trudge forth, fearful of becoming more fully awake to the possibilities that lie within and around us; for to wake up from a lifelong coma is to confront all that we are not. And that is something the mind fears even if the soul longs for it.

In my previous book, *Living an Uncommon Life*, I touched on the self-imposed move that took place in 1996, when all the doors in Chicago closed, and the only one that remained open seemed to point north. The details of this process do not seem as important as they were twelve years ago. And truth be told, so many things that look to be *ominous* turn out to be a *promise* when reflected on years later. With all that said, though, moving from our hometown to a small motel three hundred miles away without knowing how I would provide for my family or find my way in the world stretched my mental boundaries to their limits.

The journey north was based solely on a recurring vision shown to me by my subconscious mind in the six months before the move. This vision was usually accompanied by a feeling that ran across my forehead, almost as if someone were lightly dragging his finger across my skin, like a zipper being moved from closed to open. My metaphysical friends tell me that my "third eye" was being awakened, forcing me to see inside myself that which was coming. Whatever the reason, I have this mental image permanently burned into my brain. I am walking on a curved piece of road with a backpack on. There are pine trees on my right, and the sun is setting to my left. The vision lasts only a moment, and then I awaken from sleep. It was during one of those fleeting moments that I knew it was time to move on. That, and fact that this little "movie" played over and over again.

Just a couple of weeks after the move—when we were somewhat settled, with the kids enrolled in school and Jackie working—I sat in rooms 9 and 10 at the Hillcrest Motel just outside of Rapid River, Nowhere, wondering how I got myself into this mess and, more importantly, how I was going to get myself out. The connections and job skills that worked for me in Chicago did not seem to fit in my new locale. I pondered deeply the direction in which my life was supposed to go. When the vision appeared again, I knew that "the walk" would take place. I knew neither the how nor the why, but began to blindly trust the process that would eventually have four other men join me on the trip. Two began the walk with me: Duane Kinnart and Joe Johnson. Then my father-in-law, Mickey Skaja, drove backup on the trip and walked when Joe could not. On the return leg of the journey,

I walked solo, accompanied on the last few days of my adventure by Bruce Hardwick—the Ojibwa elder who predicted all of this.

While all of this seems like it happened a million years ago, the walk and the lessons it imparted (though not always fully learned) are only a moment or two away in my mind. Nowadays, I drive that same route (for the most part) to Chicago and back on a weekly basis, and it seems like every tree and blade of grass holds my footprints. I recall what I was thinking each step of the way. And whenever I pass through the town of Brookside, Wisconsin, I clearly remember the moments I shared with a small turtle that changed the direction of my life.

We had been walking straight south for about five days along the coastline of Little Bay DeNoc which turns into the western shoreline of Lake Michigan. By the time we reached Brookside, 108 miles from Rapid River, the early winds of winter were making their presence known. Our little band decided to take a lunch break, so we pulled off the main highway into a frontage road that led to a small cemetery on a hill that was dotted with headstones and had a clump of trees at the center. The wind had a real snap to it. The sun was out, but still it seemed like a good idea to use the trees as a windbreak while we ate lunch.

For some reason, I have always been—for lack of a better word—fascinated by cemeteries. Each headstone tells a very short story, and as the years have rolled on, people have taken to making grave markers reflections of those who have passed away. Pictures, inscriptions, and engravings depict the interests of the departed. In many ways, we are following what the ancient Egyptians did for their dead—adorning the site with all the mementos that meant something to the person in life. But this was a very old burial ground with markers dating back to the 1800s, when the life span of most people barely reached into their fifties and so many children never made it past their fifth birthday. As we walked through the gravesites looking for a place to sit, I felt as I always do in the presence of death—very grateful to still be upright and breathing.

Duane and I picked a spot under a very large pine tree and sat against its massive trunk out of the wind. We opened a couple of snack bars and a few bags of nuts and took a load off. We had already walked eight miles by that point and had another eight to go, so it was good to give our feet some rest. As I took off my shoes and stretched my feet out on the bed of pine needles, I noticed a small black clump that seemed to be making its way through the leaves just inches from my feet. I pulled back the dead leaves, expecting to see a mouse seeking shelter from the cold, but it was not a rodent. It was a small box turtle!

I was shocked to see the little turtle for two reasons. First, what the heck was a turtle doing in the middle of a cemetery? And, second, what the heck was a turtle doing aboveground in the middle of October? For some reason, I thought that turtles burrow underground when it's cold and stay there until the earth warms up. But if that is true, someone forgot to tell this little guy that it would be snowing very soon. As if oblivious to that information, he trudged on in a southward direction as fast as his stubby legs would take him.

Just about a quarter-mile north of where we sat, a river bends its way near the road. It occurred to me that the turtle must have been trying to make its way back to the water and was obviously going in the wrong direction—a direction that would surely lead to its eventual demise on the highway. In an instant, I thought that fate must have put the turtle in my path so I could return it to its rightful place and ensure that it would live to see another spring!

Without saying a word, I leapt to my feet, grabbed my shoes, and descended on the little turtle that had by now crawled five yards or so away. It was roughly five or six inches long, and the moment I picked it up, it hissed and "turtled up," pulling its head and legs into its knobby shell. I started back north through the cemetery and down the hill. I crossed a small gravel drive, went through another twenty yards of grass, and then walked across the frontage road and over the guardrail. Finally, I went down the embankment right to the river's edge. I held the turtle in my hand for a few minutes, examining and marveling at its engineering—its ability to carry its home on its back—and then placed the turtle just enough into the current to give it a head start to its watery world . . . freedom!

The turtle just sat there. I stood there waiting. The turtle did not move at all.

Then, as if making sure the coast was clear, out came his head, bobbing from side to side. Then one leg appeared, and then another and so on. I watched intently, feeling very God-like as I had returned one of Earth's creatures to its rightful place far away from some roadkill menu. Just then, the little reptile made an abrupt U-turn and started heading south again—across the little sand beach and toward the very embankment that I had stumbled down to get him home!

I was dumbstruck! What was this turtle's problem? Didn't it know where it belonged? Did it not know that turtles are supposed to be in or near the water? Was it not in class the day that the turtles were told they only come out of the water to bask in the sun, not walk through cemeteries in the fall? Well, I thought, if this doesn't prove that humans are the superior beings on the planet, nothing does. The turtle, of course, was not privy to my emotions and continued to churn its way up the rocky embankment.

Then, a moment changed me.

As I looked up at the steep incline and the monumental route that the little turtle was attempting, it dawned on me that it had probably taken him hours, if not a full day, to scale the side of the river, go under the guardrail, traverse the frontage road (and not become a permanent part of the asphalt), cross the twenty yards of grass (and not be grabbed by something or someone), then travel across the gravel car path and up a serious hill to cross my path just as we arrived, literally at my feet. And I, of course, in my infinite wisdom, had decided in a moment that the turtle was going in the wrong direction. I would correct the mistake and deposit him back where he *belonged*.

How many times had I done that to myself? How many times had I done that to others? As I watched the turtle struggle, I thought about my life up to that point. How many times had I pushed my way uphill, only to have someone or something send me right back down? I thought about the way the turtle pulled his head and legs into his shell for protection, even though my intent in picking him up was to help him. I thought about the fact that the turtle internally knew where it was headed—and I did not, but acted as if I did.

Ouch. It was a spiritual sliver that went right under the fingernail if there ever was one. But along with the pain was a chance for redemption! I scooped up my little, scaly buddy and leapt up the riverbank in two bounds. I jumped over the top of the guardrail and sprinted back to the spot where I had found him—or he found me—and deposited him on the very spot where I had changed the course of his life just a few minutes before.

He sat very still, and then out came his appendages and pointy head. He took a quick look around, and as if by remote control, he lifted his belly off the ground and once again motored in a southward direction through the fallen leaves and pine needles as if nothing had ever happened. I stood there in awe of this little creature that had tolerated my ignorance and absolutely knew where it was going. For a long time, I watched him make his way in and around the headstones that bore the names of souls who had made their own way in the world—short as their stay may have been—until he scurried down the other side of the hill and toward whatever place his little brain was driving him to.

We continued our walk that bone-chilling fall day to our next destination. It was a route that took a few turns in the road, but we had a map to follow that showed us the way. My four-legged friend did not need such trappings. For the rest of the afternoon, I envied the little terrapin. I wish I knew myself that well. As I put one foot in front of the other, I knew, once again, that the one who organizes all things had seen fit to let two of his creatures cross paths. The student was ready, and the teacher appeared this time as . . . a turtle.

There is a turtle shell full of teachings in this encounter. With respect to my Native American friends, I am offering to you four teachings that honor each direction. I hold the moments with this turtle as a sacred lesson, and in doing so allow for the possibility of seeing my journey as sacred, too.

Four Teachings of the Turtle

You Know the Way to Go

It may not seem like it when life is filled with all sorts of chaos (most of it created by the owner of that particular life), but somewhere deep inside you is a place that has not yet been rusted over by time, perceived failures, insults, disappointments, negativity, and fear. It comes as standard equipment at birth—CPS, or what I like to think of as a Creator Positioning System. (I would use the G-word, but it tends to scare people, start wars, and encourage people to offer up some sort of sacrifice—pretty much the opposite of what God is all about.) Each of us has this little chip inside that is made out of the same sacred stuff that G— . . . I mean, the Creator, is made of. But don't take my word for it. The Good Book says so. Go find it if you don't believe me. I'll wait . . . All set? Need more time? Sorry, time's up! It doesn't matter anyway. Either you get that you are as close to the Creator as you ever will be in this moment or you still think you need to "do" something in order to get the Almighty's attention.

The turtle, however, has no doubt about where it came from or where it's going or what it is. It's totally guided from within, unlike the majority of humans who need to hang certain types of cloth on their bodies to feel better or spend wads of dough they have not yet earned on amassing all manner of things that eventually become someone's bargain-hunting bonanza on *Antiques Roadshow* years later. If you take a moment to consider this small turtle making its way over incredible obstacles with no thought of quitting, joining a support group, or calling a talk show to complain that only the painted turtles get the breaks—and that it knew internally where it belonged and where it did not—then you have cleared the first hurdle to becoming conscious enough to move forward. Humans are the only creatures who doubt and question their existence, and by doing so, put themselves outside natural law—the law governed and run by the CPS.

Mind Your Own Business

When I plopped down under that pine tree to take a break, and Mr. Turtle (for the purpose of this piece, I am assuming he was a male turtle) crossed my path, I made his business my business in the blink of an eye. On the one hand, being a buttinsky taught me some great lessons, but on the other hand (that's why we have two hands), if I had just noticed the turtle going about its business and stayed out of its way, there would have been some value in that, as well. As well-intentioned and well-meaning as I was in the moment, my human brain took over and made all sorts of connections, assumptions, and logical calculations concerning the turtle and its path. Without being *asked,* I jumped in and made some major course corrections based on all the great knowledge I had accumulated over the years on turtles. And, of course, being an expert on the turtle, in particular, I felt perfectly justified in my actions. *Yeeeeccccchhh*—what an extra-large load of crap.

One thing about humans is that the ones who try to change the course you're on are usually just like I was that windy fall day— well-meaning. But here's the deal—they are seeing your life through *their* filters. They are running your stuff through their memory banks. They are washing your laundry in their machine— without asking or separating the colors. Thank them for caring so much and then move on. And if you have the same amount of courage that a small reptile has to launch itself on what must have felt like a cross-country trek and have been spending your business in someone else's business, stop it, plain and simple. There is an allotted time that you have stamped in your spiritual DNA that determines when you arrive and depart from this life, and I am always amazed that so many people feel they have so much extra time to talk about someone else's life, which usually indicates that theirs is totally devoid of any real meaning. Be a better human than that—or go find a turtle to teach you what's what.

Honor Their Path (and Yours)

One of the best ways to mind your own business is to be about the difficult task of honoring another's path, even if you think they are going the wrong way. In the end, of course, the turtle knew where he was going, and I obviously did not. To watch someone for whom you care deeply go down a path that, by all indications, is negative or not good for them is a major challenge. As the parent of two young adults, I grapple every day with the penchant to step in when I see what I deem is a step in the wrong direction. However, as the old adage goes, *that which hurts instructs.* I am not suggesting that we deliberately put ourselves in harm's way. But we humans as a species seem to learn more from our *hurts* (which can take a long time) than we do from our *hits* (which we tend to "skip" over and downplay). No one—often not even the person involved in a "situation"—can predict what life-changing lesson or opportunity will come out of what seems to be a bad move at the surface.

History is filled with men and women whose lives were changed for the better when things looked the darkest. If you dig into the biographies of some of our most successful leaders, you will most likely find a time or ten when a situation appeared that challenged them to move up to the next level. It was only by going through the difficult times that the better times showed up.

In the classic *Think and Grow Rich,* Napoleon Hill alluded to the presence of an "unseen Guide" whose sole purpose is to put all manner of obstacles in our path, with only one of two results. Either we become stronger and develop persistence, patience, and a burning desire to succeed with a strong inner sense of purpose, or the challenge makes us weak, fearful, impatient, and have little sense of direction or purpose in life. The bottom line is that what seems to be a setback is actually a set*up,* if we choose to see it that way. It's not a perspective that happens right away—and some take longer than others to acquire it—but the only way we can develop that insight is to navigate the potholes of life, perfectly laid out for us to deal with sooner or later. So, the next time you feel like imparting your seven cents worth, don't, unless you are asked directly.

Turtle Up and In

Look within when things get tough or someone comes along and decides to grab you by the shell and stick your nose in the dirt. There are metaphors galore about the protection a turtle carries around and how each of us has a shell to keep the outside out. And so it goes that the safest place then is within. But, unfortunately for most humans, it is the darkest, scariest, and least likely place they want to hang out. Why? Because all of our perceived failures and faults lie in the deep recesses of our being, stored away in vaults for which only we have the key. We are unwilling to unlock the door for fear that all of "it" is real and will flood over us, sending our lives into some sort of oblivion. The sad thing is that we have become our own judge, jury, and jailer without a fair trial. The CPS system has been pushed aside by our BS system—all the "bull" that fits inside for us to think about and graze on. If the outer is a manifestation of the inner, then you will not have to look very far into the crystal ball of your life to see what you have been feeding on. The results will speak for themselves.

Every great teacher, master, and prophet since day one has told us the same thing: what you think about, you become. And after a jillion years—and a jillion books and a jillion seminars—one would think that the human species would "get it." Sure, we have made some progress—we don't boil people in vats of oil because we think they are witches, and last time I checked the iron maiden wasn't used in court—but we also could make the argument that as the species progresses, we have just become more sophisticated in how we torture ourselves and each other. It's great to want to change the world, but it's more important that the world not change that deep divine core that all of us have but rarely access. Go within, turtle—or go without.

I have driven by that cemetery probably one hundred times

since my turtle encounter and have stopped by a dozen times or so. Of course, as I wander through the stones, I see the spot where two species crossed paths. And I remember that the one who was supposedly given *dominion over everything* that swims, crawls, walks, or flies was knocked down a few pegs and shown that perhaps one of humanity's biggest faults is that we think we *know* everything because we *have* everything. They are not the same thing.

> *Behold the turtle. He makes progress*
> *only when he sticks his neck out.*
> —JAMES BRYANT CONANT (1893–1978)

Just a Moment . . .

One of the great things about special moments is that you never really know when or where they are going to show up, but when they make their appearance, you can often look back at the connect-a-dots that created them. Before you close this book, I thought I would share one more.

Just a few days ago, I was home in Upper Michigan for some R&R, and on my to-do list was a stem-to-stern physical in preparation for an upcoming surgery to correct my deviated septum. After checking that all my parts were working, the doctor asked if I had ever used a prescription sinus reliever. I had not, and he suggested I do so for about a month before making the decision to have my schnozzle twisted. I relented and stopped by the local drugstore on the way home to fill the prescription. The woman at the counter greeted me with a hearty "Hi, John!" I have come to the conclusion that after years on the radio, a fair share of television interviews, and being on a book cover, more people now know who I am than I know who they are, which still takes me by surprise.

Anyway, I filled the fifteen minutes or so waiting for the prescription by purchasing some man essentials—you know, a University of Michigan rug that will fit perfectly in front of the sink in my Chicago dwelling, two different kinds of Tylenol (just in case), a few packets of highly processed turkey for a buck each, and a giant water to wash it down. When I came back to pick up the nose spray (which, by the way, has worked wonders and put off my surgery), my new friend behind the counter said plainly, "I want to thank you for changing my life."

I could sense another moment to remember coming up . . .

"How's that?" I asked.

"Well, I listened to your radio show back in 1997 and every day until you left to go on the Oprah Channel. The conversations you had, the people you talked with, the messages that you gave me changed my life for the better. I never missed a show, and I never thought I would have a chance to thank you."

Immediately, I thought of all the challenges and changes my life had to go through for that first show to get on the air, not to mention the thousands that followed over the years. "It was my pleasure and honor to sit behind the microphone and know that it mattered," I told her.

"That's not the end of it!" she said. "After not hearing your show for a time, I got a bit depressed, but one day I thought to myself, *if he could do it, so could I!* So, I called the radio station you started at, made an appointment, told them my story (Alice Sabuco, this means you!) and asked for my chance to be on the air."

"And . . . ," I prompted.

"I have my own show every third Monday for thirty minutes in the morning!"

I didn't know what to say . . . talk about a full-circle moment!

"So, can I be a guest on your show?" I asked.

"Oh, my," she said, "what would we talk about?"

"How every moment matters," I answered.

Since I first began writing this book in June 2007, my daughter has graduated from high school and finished her second year of college. (The whole college thing is another book.) My son, who was a sophomore when I started this, is months away from leaving the high-school experience and seeing what the world has to offer. Two more season cycles have come and gone, along with friends who have passed away and some new additions to the human family. I started writing on that cool summer morning at the age of forty-eight, and now as I wrap up my latest rant in winter, fifty is my new biological age. The economy has tanked and we have a new president, but the fervor of his inauguration has passed and both sides seem to be entrenched in politics as usual. Ah, nothing like change. I had to wait over the past two years for some of the moments in this book to happen; they were not part of the original lineup as it were. *Patience* is the key word here, and allowing the process to serve up moments that, for whatever reason, needed to be included in the book, perhaps just so you could read it.

As late winter turns to spring, my thoughts turn to being outside and baseball in particular—the one thing I can count on that allows me to forget the chaos of the world (for a few hours) and feel like a kid again. The upcoming Chicago Cubs season holds little or no promise, but rest assured that my rear will be in a seat because, when it comes down to it, it's not about what's on the scoreboard. I know that when I walk into the concrete shrine called Wrigley Field and ascend the steps to the entrance of the seats, when I can see that expanse of green, splashed by the summer sun, and the stands filled with color and the smell of hot dogs in the air, in that *moment* I know that I am alive. My hope is that you have a place that does the same for you.

This last page is a reminder that you have an expiration date stamped somewhere in your DNA. The average person spends about ten years of his life watching television . . . ten years! Imagine if you could use that time to grasp all the opportunities you have to change the world. We have a lifetime of moments to spend with the hungry who need to be fed, those who are lost and walk the streets of our cities, struggling readers in after-school programs, the elderly and shut-ins looking for a hand to hold, abused animals that need to be cared for, children in need of a Big Brother or Big Sister who can make or break their spirit, or our own kids just playing catch. There are a million more ways to make the most of the moments you have left before your time here on Earth expires.

John Denver, a man whose expiration date came up too soon, wrote, "The moment at hand is the only thing we really own." Let me add that the moment at hand is also the only thing we can create *more of and contribute to by being aware of its existence.* This book started out with a definition of a moment from *Webster's Dictionary,* but the truth is that the only person who really gets to define whether a moment has meaning—or is a waste of time—is *you.*

Life is made of millions of moments, but we live only
one of these moments at a time. As we begin to
change this moment, we begin to change our lives.
—D. TRINIDAD HUNT

About the Author

John St. Augustine has been called "the voice of America" by veteran broadcaster Charles Osgood and "the most influential voice on radio" by best-selling author Cheryl Richardson. He is the creator and host of the nationally syndicated Power!Talk Radio, a radio show that brings together a viewing of points that empowers listeners with a renewed sense of life's possibilities. In June, 2006 St. Augustine helped launch the Oprah & Friends XM Satellite Radio network, and now over 750,000 people a day hear his daily nationally syndicated radio vignette *Powerthoughts!* on the channel In 2007, *The Jean Chatzky Show* won the coveted Gracie Allen Award under his leadership. He is currently the senior producer of *The Dr. Oz Show*. John is the author of *Living An Uncommon Life: Essential Lessons from 21 Extraordinary People* and a contributor to the *Chicken Soup for the Soul* series. He is a graduate of Northeastern Illinois University and a veteran of the United States Coast Guard. He calls both Chicago and Upper Michigan home.

Hampton Roads Publishing Company

. . . for the evolving human spirit

HAMPTON ROADS PUBLISHING COMPANY
publishes books on a variety of subjects,
including spirituality, health, and other
related topics.

For a copy of our latest trade catalog,
call 978-465-0504 or
visit our website at www.hrpub.com